American Baskets

American Baskets

Robert Shaw

Clarkson Potter/Publishers
New York

preceding pages:

DEGIKUP (DETAIL)

Louisa Keyser (Washo). 1917–1918. Carson City, Nevada. Willow, bracken fern, redbud. H: 12", D: 16¼". Philbrook Museum of Art, Tulsa, Oklahoma, Clark Field Collection.

Keyser's degikups are among the most tightly sewn coiled baskets ever made. This masterpiece of the basketmaker's art has thirty stitches per inch.

opposite: SET OF SEVENTEEN NESTING BASKETS

Daryl and Karen Arawjo. 1995. Bushkill, Pennsylvania. Handsplit white oak with walnut bases. Smallest basket ½" diameter; largest 14" diameter.

This virtuoso contemporary nested set is woven with white oak splint rather than rattan, but otherwise follows traditional Nantucket style.

FIELD BASKET (DETAIL)

Artist unknown. c. 1860. New England. Painted black ash splint with carved hardwood handles. Overall height: 16"; diameter 20". Photograph courtesy David A. Schorsch American Antiques.

New England farmers used deep round baskets like this to harvest corn, potatoes, and other heavy crops. Paint was not only decorative but also protected hard-used outdoor baskets from rot. The unusually long tails of the handles extend to the base of the basket.

opposite: GIFT BASKETS

Pomo. c. 1900. Central California. Coiled grass decorated with feathers, beads, and shells. Field Museum of Natural History, Chicago. Trans. #A106760c; cat. #71570. Photograph by John Weinstein.

Pomo women tucked feathers into their baskets while they were sewing them so that they became an integral part of the structure. A single basket might take a year or more to complete and could incorporate hundreds of tiny feathers plucked from the skins of several different species.

Published by Clarkson Potter/Publishers, New York, New York. Member of the Crown Publishing Group.

Random House, Inc. New York, Toronto, London, Sydney, Auckland www.randomhouse.com

CLARKSON N. POTTER is a trademark and POTTER and colophon are registered trademarks of Random House, Inc.

Printed in China

Design by Maggie Hinders

Library of Congress Cataloging-in-Publication Data
    Shaw, Robert, 1951–
    American baskets / Robert Shaw. — 1st ed.
    Includes bibliographical references and index.
1. Baskets—United States. I. Title.
NK3649.55.U6S52   1999
746.41'2'0973—dc21   98-48680

ISBN 0-609-60333-7

10 9 8 7 6 5 4 3 2 1

First Edition

To my girls: Nancy, Emma, Georgia, and Lily

Acknowledgments

THIS BOOK would not have been possible without the generosity, assistance, and talents of many people. Special thanks are due to my dear friends the late Harold Corbin and his wife Florie, who got me started on this subject many years ago in the basket-filled loft of their barn in Salisbury, Connecticut. I am also especially indebted to collectors and historians Roddy Moore, Nellie Ptasvek, and Cynthia Taylor, who graciously loaned baskets for photography and provided reams of helpful information, and to Ken Burris, who took superb photographs of these and other baskets especially for the book. Thanks also to Larry Hackley, Paul Madden, and the late Allan Lobb, who allowed me to use photos of baskets from their great collections, and to Nantucket basket historian David Wood, who gave me many helpful pieces of information and arranged photography of several superb island baskets.

In addition to Cynthia Taylor, I am also indebted to master basket-makers Daryl and Karen Arawjo, Denise Davis, Thelma Hibdon, Mary Jackson, Gerrie Kennedy, Jonathan Kline, Tom and Connie McColley, John McGuire, Joyce Schaum, Marie Elena Stotler, Billy Ruth Suddoth, Velveeta Volante, Martha Wetherbee, Aaron Yakim, and Stephen Zeh, all of whom helped me better understand the history, attitudes, and processes of traditional basketmaking in America.

Thanks also to Judith Sellars, manager of archival collections, Museum of New Mexico; Tommy Hines, executive director, Shaker Museum at South Union; Martha Labell, Photographic Archives, Peabody Museum of Archaeology and Ethnology, Harvard University; Julie M. Sowell, curator, The Appalachian Museum at Berea College; Rip Gerry of the Haffenreffer Museum of Anthropology, Brown University; Tommie Rodgers, registrar/curator of collections, Lauren Rogers Museum of Art, Rebecca Cole-Will, curator, The Abbe Museum; Sara Greensfelder, president of the California Indian Basketweavers Association; Paul and Elaine Rocheleau; Brian Cullity; Don Carpentier; Ellin Silberblatt and Hugh Lauter Levin of Levin Associates in Southport, Connecticut; Mimi Handler, editor of *Early American Homes* magazine and champion of traditional craftsmanship; Russell Hartman, curator of anthropology at the California Academy of Sciences; Sandra Staebell of the Kentucky Museum, Western Kentucky University: Allison Eckhardt Ledes, editor, *The Magazine Antiques;* David A. Schorsch; Philip Zea, deputy director and curator, Historic Deerfield; Edwin Churchill, chief curator, Maine State Museum; Richard Rasso; Sally Moore Majewski, director of marketing and development, Hancock Shaker Village; Robin Woodward of the Shelburne Museum: Mary Elizabeth Woodruff, photo archivist, Nantucket Historical Association; Dr. Christopher Marshall, Unity College in Maine; Mary Giles, assistant archivist, The Charleston Museum; Kim Walters, library director, Braun Research Library, The Southwest Museum; Emory S. Campbell, director, The Penn Center, Inc., St. Helena, South Carolina; Jerry Zollars, director of events, Southwestern Association for Indian Arts, Inc., Santa Fe; and Richard A. Shrader, reference archivist, The Academic Libraries, University of North Carolina at Chapel Hill.

Grateful thanks to everyone at Clarkson Potter: editors Kathryn Crosby and Christopher Smith, copy editor Donna Ryan, editorial director Lauren Shakely, and designer Maggie Hinders.

Finally, thanks to my daughters, Emma and Georgia, who, as usual, pointed out their favorites without hesitation, and to my wife, Nancy, who lovingly supported me and the project across many, many hills and valleys.

Robert Shaw
Shelburne, Vermont

below: FEATHER BASKET
Jonathan Kline. 1995. Trumansburg, New York. Black ash. Private collection.
Like full-size versions of this traditional form, this diminutive basket's lid slides up and down on the handle.

following page: BERRY BASKET (DETAIL)
Unknown Indian artist. c. 1890. New England. Painted wood splint with carved hardwood handle. H: 5½", W: 4¼", L: 4¼". Private collection. Photograph courtesy David A. Schorsch American Antiques.
A simple, colorfully painted Indian-made example of a type common throughout New England and used to gather the region's abundant and delicious wild berries. In both Indian and white communities, families and friends often gathered together to harvest wild strawberries in June, blueberries in July, and raspberries and blackberries in August.

Contents

Introduction   13

Part I: NATIVE AMERICAN TRADITIONS   29

  The Aleuts of Alaska   31

  The Pacific Northwest   37

  California and the Great Basin   49

  The Southwest   67

  The Southeast   77

  The Northeast   87

Part II: IMMIGRANT TRADITIONS   99

  New England   101

  The Shakers   119

  The Taconic Area   135

  Nantucket   143

  The Pennsylvania Dutch and Other Germans   155

  Appalachia   163

  African-Americans of the Southeast Coast   187

Collecting and Caring for Baskets   199

Selected Resources   207

Notes   211

For Further Reading   212

Glossary   214

Index   215

Introduction

HANDMADE BASKETS were once among the most common of domestic objects; for nearly ten thousand years they were an integral and virtually invisible part of the daily life of people all over North America. Whether in a Native American village, around a small New England hill farm, or in the fields of a vast southern plantation, baskets were essential tools, so closely tied to work that their names encompass the scope of home and agricultural activities. Berry baskets, sewing baskets, feather baskets, parching baskets, clam baskets, gathering baskets, apple baskets, lunch baskets, potato baskets, winnowing baskets, laundry baskets, market baskets, storage baskets, pack baskets, bread-rising baskets, cheese baskets, burden baskets, tray baskets, gathering baskets, and egg baskets—all had their place within the daily round of chores. Searching local woods and fields, skilled basketmakers gathered grasses, strips of split wood or cane, twigs, vines, tree bark, and other materials that could be woven, twisted, or coiled into the forms they needed. Using only the simplest of tools to aid them in gathering and shaping the raw material, these artisans often created works of enduring beauty and artistry, everyday masterpieces that transcend their own time and purpose.

Baskets and basketmaking have long since lost their central place in our country's cultures, however. Handmade baskets have been almost entirely supplanted in the twentieth century by mass-produced containers, which are usually made of synthetic materials. The wastebaskets, clothes hampers, and laundry baskets we use every day are imitation baskets only, made of inexpensive molded plastic rather than handwoven natural fibers. We hang graduated wire-mesh baskets beside the kitchen sink to hold sponges, brushes, and soaps or ripening fruits and vegetables; we organize the files and letters on our desks in plastic or metal racks; and we tote our groceries, yesterday's newspapers, household trash, and fallen leaves in disposable plastic bags. If we do have wooden baskets in our homes, they were made not by a local artisan but by foreign craftspeople working where hand labor is still cheap and affordable to the mass marketers who supply such goods. Unfortunately, price, not quality, is often the measure in today's throwaway society, where handmade baskets must compete favorably with less expensive machine-made products.

Paradoxically, however, the cachet of older handmade baskets has never been higher. Indeed, despite their original humble functions in and

opposite: SEWING BASKET
John McGuire. 1997. Geneva, New York. Ebony, leather, cherry base, brass, corian, cane, white oak, waxed linen. H: 5", D: 10" Private collection.
The oak staves of this contemporary Nantucket-style basket are inserted in a solid cherry base. The lid, which has lashed and nailed rims, was woven on a traditional form and is hinged with cane-wrapped leather.

around the home, time and vast social changes have turned many old baskets into collector's items. Collectors appreciate fine antique baskets for their history, form, color, and craftsmanship, and many seek out traditional baskets by outstanding contemporary craftspeople for use as decorative and artful accents in their homes. Handmade baskets have also become a fixture of the popular country-style decor featured in countless magazines since the bicentennial. They serve, in part, as nostalgic symbols of the simpler, self-reliant values of a cherished, if romanticized, early America, and as emblems of this country's small-town, agricultural past. Similarly, historic Native American baskets can provide connections to the now esteemed American Indian cultures, acting as windows into their remote, exotic, and largely vanished ways of life.

In the context of a consumer-oriented society, when seemingly every need is met with inexpensive, anonymously manufactured imported goods, baskets are also valued as examples of locally produced, preindustrial handcraftsmanship. They exemplify the pride of workmanship and the accountability of members of the community in earlier times. A fine handmade basket, whether new or old, speaks of the time, skill, and care that have gone into its making and proclaims that use and beauty can be complementary rather than mutually exclusive, as so often seems the case in today's utilitarian objects. Baskets can connote a time before the dawn of industrial capitalism, before American lives were forever changed and "simplified" by the advent of such powerful (and surprisingly recent) inventions as the telephone, the automobile, and electric light and power, let alone radio, television, and personal computers. Perhaps more than anything else, handmade baskets suggest an approach to time far different from today's frenzied pace. As the renowned contemporary textile designer and basketmaker Ed Rossbach has pointed out,

> The basketmaking process induces not only meditation and contemplation, but an unusual awareness of time, a celebration, an observation. . . . When a person says, upon looking at a basket, "Think of the time it took to make it," he may be doing more than merely illuminating the distorted values which are part of the detestable illness of the century, that anything which takes time is not worth bothering with. It has become essential to feel a pres-

above: RATTLE LID BASKET
Tlingit. c. 1910. Southeastern Alaska. Spruce root, bear grass and maidenhair fern, probably colored with aniline dyes. D: 8½". Peabody Museum of Archaeology and Ethnology, Harvard University, Cambridge, Massachusetts. Photograph by Hillel Burger.
This relatively brightly colored basket was probably made for the tourist trade.

sure of time, to reject anything which requires an abundance of time. And with such a rejection of doing ourselves, we reject any full appreciation of what others are doing or have done. Yet by feeling "time" when he confronts a piece of quilting or embroidery or lacemaking or basketry, the viewer may be close to the essence of the art.[1]

Basketmaking is an ancient American tradition, with roots that may extend to the very beginning of New World civilization itself. Native Americans created some of the oldest known baskets in the world before the arrival of Europeans. Archaeologists in the early years of the twentieth century first discovered these prehistoric baskets preserved in remarkable numbers in the arid desert climate of the Great Basin of Utah and Nevada. Crafted and used by members of the region's archaic Desert Culture, they may have been made more than ten thousand years ago. The relative sophis-

above: STORAGE BASKET

Unknown Penobscot artist. c. 1830. Maine. Black ash splint with carved hardwood handles. H: 18", D: 24". Mary C. Wheelwright Collection, Abbe Museum, Bar Harbor, Maine. Photograph by Stephen Bicknell.

The complexity of making round bottoms vexed many early Indian artisans, so this basket combines a square bottom with a round top. The extremely fine weavers are also typical of early nineteenth-century Maine Indian work. Early basketmakers peddled baskets like these door-to-door, a practice later made unnecessary by the development of the tourist trade.

tication of these early baskets suggests that the craft was not a new one, but that it had probably been practiced for centuries. Some anthropologists have suggested that basketry may have come to the New World with the first humans who crossed the Arctic bridge from the Siberian peninsula.

From these ancient beginnings, the making and use of baskets can be traced through virtually every society and cultural group that has ever inhabited North America. While other Native American crafts, such as pottery, weaving, beadwork, and wood carving, found widely scattered adherents, nearly all American Indian tribes made baskets; in many of those societies, baskets were the dominant handcraft. Once established, basketry traditions changed relatively little over time, especially in the centuries before contact with Europeans totally disrupted Indian societies. Some Native American basket traditions can be traced in a direct and continuous lineage over hundreds or even thousands of years. Well-preserved Anasazi baskets from the Southwest, for example, made between the birth of Christ and about A.D. 700, are hard to distinguish from Pima baskets made in the late nineteenth and early twentieth centuries.

Basketmaking is not only an ancient and widespread Native American tradition but also an extraordinarily rich one. The relative simplicity of basketmaking's basic techniques made it accessible to many artisans and allowed Native Americans to achieve and maintain an impressive early standard of quality in the craft. American Indians are generally acknowledged to have produced the most varied, technically advanced, and aesthetically significant baskets of any civilization in history. The achievements of such culturally diverse tribes as Alaska's Aleut, California's Pomo, Nevada's Washo, and Louisiana's Chitimacha are unparalleled and must be considered among the great accomplishments of American craftsmanship and design.

But Indians were by no means America's only outstanding basketmakers. Adding to the extraordinary depth and stature of America's basketmaking heritage are the strong and distinctive traditions developed during the eighteenth and nineteenth centuries by African-American slaves in coastal South Carolina and Georgia; by German immigrants in Pennsylvania and Virginia; by Shaker brethren in New York, New England, Ohio, and Kentucky; by Scots-Irish descendants in southern Appalachia; by the Yankee farmers of New England; and by the lightship crews who guarded the treacherous shoals off Nantucket Island. All of these immigrants brought influences from their own cultures to the practice of basketry in the New World, combining America's raw materials with their own often venerable traditions. Basket forms and construction methods preserved throughout the eighteenth, nineteenth, and early twentieth centuries in the archaic African-American Gullah culture of the South Carolina and Georgia coast and sea islands, for example, can be traced to origins in west central Africa, while historic Pennsylvania Dutch baskets clearly show the influence of vintage German, Swiss, and Alsatian coiled-straw models. Native American and immigrant cultures also interacted in the New World, particularly in the Northeast, where Indian and European basket makers traded ideas and influences for hundreds of years.

After the necessary first step of toolmaking and perhaps the related textile arts of twining rope and netting, basketry is the most ancient of human crafts. It is also the most basic of all crafts in its methods and materials. Basketmaking is a local art, not dependent on foreign or specially processed materials of any kind. Its twin and only possible rival in age is pottery, a far more complex craft that most historians and archaeologists now believe evolved from basketmaking. Almost certainly the two crafts

following pages: WORK BASKET
Artist unknown. c. 1880. New England. Black ash, hardwood handles. H: 9½", D: 24". Shelburne Museum, Shelburne, Vermont. Photograph by Ken Burris.
A sturdy and extremely well-crafted basket with dozens of uses around the farm.

intersected and influenced each other early in their parallel development. Basketry and pottery serve many of the same utilitarian functions and often share similar or even identical forms and decorative motifs within a society or region. Southwest Indians, for example, made distinctive large storage vessels known as ollas from both clay and fiber and decorated them with related abstract geometric motifs. In this case the baskets taking this form came long after the pottery, but cause and effect are not always so obvious.

Fired clay pots have the decided advantage of being nonporous, although some Indian baskets were woven so tightly that they too could hold liquids. Ceramic pots are far more durable than baskets, which are completely biodegradable and decompose over time under the influence of the elements. For this reason, far more pots than early baskets are still extant. However, a number of very old pots exist that bear the outside imprints of woven basket containers, supporting the assumption that baskets came first and were used as molds or models to form some of the earliest pieces of pottery.

In early Native American societies, as in many hunting and gathering cultures, women served as artisans and saw to child care and the gathering, preparation, cooking, and storage of vegetables, grains, fruits, and nuts. Almost invariably, the women were the basketmakers, weaving plant fibers such as shoots, reeds, and grasses into containers for specific purposes.

Baskets were especially important to agricultural societies, whose settled way of life allowed the development of complex religions, rituals, and arts. Basketmaking and agriculture progressed together; with the development of agriculture came permanent, structured settlements, capable of supporting hundreds or even thousands of people. Native American craftspeople developed practical basket forms to fit the varied tasks of farming, such as sowing, watering, harvesting, winnowing, grinding, mixing, and storing seeds and crops. Many varieties of agricultural baskets were later made by the European immigrants who settled the fertile lands of the New World.

Although they can be manipulated in extremely complex ways by a master artisan, the basic techniques of basketmaking are simple and easy to learn. From the earliest times, artisans have used three basic basketmaking techniques: plaiting, twining, and coiling. Probably the most familiar

left: SEAGRASS BASKETMAKERS
at work along the roadside in Mount
Pleasant, South Carolina, c. 1985.
*Folklife Resource Center, McKissick Museum,
University of South Carolina, Columbia, South
Carolina.*

method, practiced by artisans throughout the eastern United States, is
plaiting, which involves weaving flat pliable horizontal strips (the weft)
over and under sturdier vertical elements (the warp), which serve as the
basic framework of the basket. By using the second technique, twining,
the basketmaker creates a finer and more elaborate weave structure by
twisting two or more strands of thin, flexible weft around the vertical
warp elements, which are also usually thin. Twining was most widely
practiced among the Indian tribes of northern California and the Pacific
Northwest. Coiling, the third method, was popular among the California,
Great Basin, and southwestern Indians as well as among slaves and their
descendants in the southeast coastal lowlands. It differs from plaiting and
twining in that it is basically a sewing rather than a weaving technique.
Round in form, coiled baskets are made by forming a continuous spiral
with bunched grass or other plant strands and then stitching the resulting
coils together.

Baskets are handcrafted objects, generally produced by a single artisan
who oversees and manipulates the process from start to finish. The

craftsperson requires only the simplest of tools, often no more than a knife to cut raw materials or to shape a handle. No other craft is so directly connected with the hands of its creator; in woven basketmaking not even a sewing needle intercedes between the craftsperson and the medium. Unlike pottery, which depends for success upon heat to harden the clay and the glazes, basketmaking depends only on the quality of the materials and the skill of the craftsperson.

Basketry is also more closely linked with its source materials than most other handcrafts. The basketmaker gathers and prepares her own materials, usually from nearby woods and fields, and then shapes them by hand into finished form. She may choose to embellish her basket with paint, dyed fibers, feathers, shells, or other common and locally available materials. Baskets served to connect their makers and users with the natural world from which the materials came. The basketmaker, in effect, created her work out of the natural world, transforming wild, uncultivated plants into useful objects. She lived close to nature and developed an intimate knowledge of the plants she used in crafting her baskets. She knew which trees and grasses provided the best material, where and when to look for them, how to prepare and season them for use, and how to manipulate them into the forms and designs she sought to create.

Baskets are also intimate and tactile objects, made in human scale to fit comfortably into the hands or against the bodies of their users. The double-curved base of a ribbed buttocks basket nestles perfectly over a leg; an oval or rectangular work basket fits comfortably into or across the lap; a flat-sided egg basket can be hugged tight against the side; a winnowing tray is held between outstretched arms. Some baskets were even made to be worn. Northwest coast Indians, for instance, made cone-shaped basket hats to keep out the region's almost perpetual rain; southwestern women created vase-shaped jars, which they balanced on their heads when gathering seeds; and Indians and whites in many parts of the country made pack or burden baskets in which to carry food and possessions on their backs.

Many Native Americans also created ceremonial baskets used in seasonal rituals or rites of passage. Hopi Indians, for example, still make baskets that are carried in the wedding procession and remain with the bride and groom throughout their life together. These baskets are buried with their owners because they are believed to help transport the soul between

opposite: COVERED FANCY BASKET (DETAIL)
Elizabeth Conrad Hickox (Wiyot/Karok). c. 1920. Klamath River area, northwestern California. Twined hazel shoots, beargrass, maidenhair fern, and dyed porcupine quills. H: 7¼", D: 5½". Lauren Rogers Museum of Art, Laurel, Mississippi. Gift of Catherine Marshall Gardiner. This typically masterful example of Hickox's work is woven with seventeen stitches per inch. She created the decorative pattern by combining false-embroidered dark brown maidenhair fern stems with porcupine quills that had been dyed yellow with oak tree lichen. Indians dried dull white and tan porcupine quills before dyeing them. Women chewed the three-to-five-inch-long quills to soften them, then flattened and wove them into place with a needle. Quills were far more commonly used to decorate leather clothing, moccasins, and pouches than baskets, and their use was an anacronism by Hickox's time.

this world and the next. Many Indian baskets, utilitarian and ceremonial alike, were decorated with symbols that were passed down within particular tribes or regional cultures. The Pomo of California, for example, are renowned for their masterful gift baskets, made as presents for important people or as items of exchange among women of the tribe. The jewel-like baskets are elaborately decorated with shells and bright feathers that symbolize pride, love, fidelity, courage, and a host of other spiritual qualities.

While the nineteenth century saw the rise of professional basketmakers who produced multiple copies of a form for sale, most earlier baskets were made in small numbers by those who intended to use them. All traditional basketry evokes a lost world, harder and smaller than the present one, but more directly in contact with the natural world and the ageless rhythms of the earth and seasons. Especially among Native Americans, basketmaking once was, as one art historian wrote, "a completely organic noncommercial activity with craft skills acquired instinctively and handed down from generation to generation so that the business of making a basket acquired a ceremonial quality, putting the maker at one with nature and its seasons. It represents the prelapsarian ideal toward which many modern craftsmen aspire."[2]

Any possibility of reaching that now self-conscious ideal has, of course, been shattered over the course of the past two centuries. Few Americans live close to the land nowadays, and baskets are no longer necessities of an agrarian way of life. However, despite the enormous historical and societal changes it has weathered, the craft of basketry remains alive and well. Even today it ranks with quilting and other forms of needlework as the most widely and continuously practiced of all traditional folk crafts. Hundreds of craftspeople all over the country —men and women of all races and cultures—carry on family and local traditions that can be traced back unbroken through several generations. Appalachia, in particular, remains a center of traditional basketmaking, with many craftspeople carrying on long traditions of white oak basketwork. Similarly, hundreds of basketmakers in the South Carolina low country centered around Mount Pleasant, just north of Charleston, carry on the three-hundred-year-old rush and sweetgrass basketmaking tradition of the region, selling their wares to tourists in city markets and shops and from stands along Highway 17. And throughout the country, Native American artisans continue to craft baskets with close ties to those of their ancestors.

Unfortunately, the humble origins and everyday functions of traditional baskets have long obscured their cultural and artistic importance. In recent years, however, scholars of folk art, material culture, and traditional craftsmanship have begun to clarify basketry's place in the history of American life and art. Museums throughout the country now regularly present exhibitions of traditional basketry, and academics such as Jeannette Lasansky of Pennsylvania, Rosemary O. Joyce of Ohio, and Sarah H. Hill of Georgia have produced studies that place baskets and basketmakers into deep and complex artistic, social, and historical contexts. In addition, a number of dedicated younger basketmakers have researched neglected traditions and brought them back to life through their work. Martha Wetherbee's extensive hands-on study of the nearly moribund Shaker basketmaking tradition, for example, has been vital to both historians and craftspeople, and her books, magazine articles, and classes have inspired hundreds of others to learn and thereby preserve the basic techniques of this important tradition. West Virginians Rachel Nash Law and Cynthia Taylor have similarly researched the region's baskets and its many still active elder artisans with the respect of cultural historians and the keen artistic eyes of master craftspeople.

Despite these efforts, the gaps between the traditional societies that have nurtured basketry and the modern technological world are difficult to bridge. Misunderstandings are inevitable when traditional and con-

opposite: CHILD'S BASKET
Artist unknown. c. 1880. Probably Connecticut. Stained white oak splint with hardwood handle. OH: 6¾", W: 6", L: 6¾". Private collection. This well-proportioned little basket has a thin, delicate handle made to fit a child's hand. Southern New England basketmakers occasionally used white oak rather than ash as their "basket stuff."

sumer cultures encounter each other, because their value systems and especially their approaches to time have almost nothing in common. Where traditional cultures value the investment of time in a task well done, modern society prizes speed above all and tends to reward individuals or methods that can accomplish the most in the shortest time. To the modern consumer looking for a bargain, the traditional artisan's refusal to cut corners seems almost perverse. As Sarah Hill puts it, "The amount of history, labor, time, and skill invested in one basket is incomprehensible to many people who visit the Cherokee reservation. One cool fall morning as I stood studying a basket display in the co-op, an indignant white woman stalked up, grasping tightly in her hand a medium-sized white oak wastebasket. . . . She shook the basket angrily and exclaimed, 'Have you seen the prices on these baskets? Don't they know we're tourists?'. . . There was no adequate response. My surprise has never been what baskets cost in the present, but rather what they cost in the past."[3]

Traditional American basketry is a paradoxically complex craft, simple in its concepts but kaleidoscopic in its variety. Its ritualized, time-honored methods have allowed an extraordinary range of expression and creativity, and its modest intentions have elicited a host of distinguished achievements. Basketmaking spans the continent, its history, and its peoples, suggesting a definition of the word American that is at once broader and more unified than any other craft can offer. No other handcraft has been an identifiable part of human society for so long or has changed so little over the centuries.

For those willing to pay attention, a traditional basket teaches respect for the American past, for our ancestors' slower, more natural rhythms, their attention to small but practical details, and their unwavering desire to integrate beauty and utility. The baskets of the Shakers and the Hopi, of the Southern Highlands and the northwest coast, can reveal the rich history of their makers' daily existence and help us understand their quietly remarkable connection to the land that sustained them for so long. Like all other forms of traditional art, basketry today is struggling to adapt to a world that no longer requires its products. In the end, the artistic and spiritual values inherent in this venerable craft may prove its most valuable assets and help to ensure its survival into the twenty-first century.

opposite: COBRA BASKET WITH HANDLE

Mary Jackson. 1984. Charleston, South Carolina. Bulrush, sweetgrass, longleaf pine needles, palmetto leaf. 16" x 16" x 12". Private collection. Photograph by Jack Alterman.

Jackson spends as long as two months crafting one of her complex, original designs and carefully manipulates her different-colored materials. Here, the lighter-colored grasses of the rim and handle and the bright diagonals and vertical lines formed by the palmetto stitches create strongly contrasting patterns on the basket's surface. Jackson named this basket form for its resemblance to a coiled fakir's snake.

following page:

FOOD BASKET (DETAIL)

Haida. Collected by Emma Shaw Colcleugh c. 1885. Queen Charlotte Islands, British Columbia. Spruce root, beargrass, maidenhair fern. H: 10", D:10". Haffenreffer Museum of Anthropology, Brown University, Bristol, Rhode Island. Photograph by Cathy Carver.
Tightly woven baskets like this were used by Northwest coast Indians to carry water and cook foods. Food was cooked by dropping red hot stones into water or meal mush.

Part I

Native American
Traditions

The Aleuts
of Alaska

above. LIDDED BASKET
Aleut. Late nineteenth century. Aleutian Islands. H: 19 cm. Rye grass with embroidered silk floss. National Museum of the American Indian, Smithsonian.
The elaborate floral designs on this basket may have been inspired by observations of late Victorian-era embroidery or cross-stitch. The basket was probably made for sale to tourists, who would have found its decoration familiar and attractive.

left: ALEUT BASKETMAKER demonstrating her craft at the Columbian Exposition in St. Louis, Missouri, 1904.
Photograph by Charles Carpenter. The Field Museum, Chicago; Neg. #13299.

opposite: GIFT BASKET
Aleut. c. 1880–1920. Probably Bristol Bay or Attu, Alaska. Twined rye grass with false embroidered worsted wool yarn and down feathers. H: 9", D: 9" Lauren Rogers Museum of Art, Laurel, Mississippi. Gift of Catherine Marshall Gardiner.
The top of this basket is edged with a looping chain of thickly braided grass. The use of eagle down feathers and the basket's virtually unused condition indicate it was intended as a gift and meant to be cherished rather than used.

preceding page: NAKOAKTOK, a Kwakiutl woman, painting a ceremonial basket hat, British Columbia, c. 1915. (Detail.)
Photograph by Edward Sheriff Curtis.

The Aleuts, a major native group of Alaskans, have long been considered among the finest basketmakers in the world. Residents of the Aleutian Islands—a chain of small, barren, fogbound, and treeless lands located 1,000 miles south of the Arctic

below: GATHERING BASKET
below: GATHERING BASKET
Aleut. c. early 1900s, Aleutian Islands. Rye grass stems (foundation and weft), wool embroidery yarn and seal intestine (design). D: 30.5 cm, H: 19.7 cm. California Academy of Sciences, San Francisco; catalog #145-15. Photograph by Dong Lin.
This relatively wide utilitarian basket is decorated with a combination of imported colored yarn and strands of dark brown seal intestine.

Circle and stretching 1,000 miles off Alaska's southwest coast toward Russia—the Aleuts lived a far more stable life than the nomadic Eskimos, who made very few baskets of aesthetic note. They lived year-round in coastal villages governed by wealthy and powerful chiefs in a highly structured and class-conscious society that included slaves as its bottom tier. Aleuts dwelled in substantial communal homes, built partially underground for insulation from the cold and damp and roofed with driftwood or whalebone covered with sod. Like the Eskimos, the Aleuts were hunters of Alaska's sea mammals, which served as their main source of food and clothing.

Eager to collect the rich fur of the plentiful seals and sea otters, Russian hunters began to traverse the Aleutians in the 1740s, bringing devastating change and oppression to the region and its people. Setting up hunting camps throughout the islands, greedy Russian fur traders decimated the Aleuts, enslaving, raping, and killing thousands of natives and dooming many thousands more with the spread of their diseases. By the time the United States acquired the Aleutian Islands as part of its Alaska purchase of 1867, the Aleut population had dropped from an estimated precontact high of around 20,000 to less than 1,000. Despite gains in this century, the Aleuts still have not recovered more than a third of that population loss.

Basketmaking was practiced by Aleutian women from the earliest times, and many ancient baskets and fragments have been uncovered in archaeological digs. Like everything else made by the natives of this harsh land, baskets were essential to survival. Aleuts used baskets to collect the eggs of seabirds and to store dried meats and berries, which sustained life through the long dark winter months of greatest scarcity. Hats and capes were also woven from grass, as were baglike wallets made to carry personal accessories, and mats used for a variety of household applications.

The traditional material for Aleutian baskets was a type of ryegrass (*Elymus mollis*) that grew wild throughout the islands and was carefully gathered and prepared over the course of several months. Harsh elements at the coast kept the grass from reaching its full maturity, so in the early summer the women traveled inland to find the longest and tough-

est grass available. The cut grass was stored indoors, away from sunlight, while it dried, and then sorted or split into extremely thin strands with a fingernail. Finally the prepared strands were bundled together and hung outside on cloudy days, to avoid the bleaching effects of sunlight, until they were completely dry and ready for use.

Aleuts fashioned their baskets by twining thin, flexible horizontal (weft) strands together between vertical (warp) elements. In twining, two or more strands of weft are twisted around each other in half turns as they pass over and under the warp elements. The Aleuts used ryegrass for both warp and weft, weaving the delicate threadlike strands of prepared grass so tightly that the texture of the finished baskets has often been compared to linen cloth. Aleuts decorated the baskets with false embroidery, created by wrapping grasses or fern stems around the weft strands while weaving, so

above: GIFT BASKETS

Aleut. Early 1900s. Aleutian Islands. Rye grass with embroidered wool yarn, silk floss and eagle down feathers. Height of right basket: 10". Peabody Museum of Archaeology and Ethnology, Harvard University, Cambridge, Massachusetts. Photograph by Hillel Burger.

Aleut baskets decorated with both false embroidered designs and fluffy eagle down feathers are extremely rare.

above: TWINED BASKET WITH LID
Aleut. c. early 1900s. Aleutian Islands. Rye grass stems (foundation and weft), silk embroidery yarn (design). D: 29 cm; height with lid: 26 cm. California Academy of Sciences, San Francisco; catalog #1994-8-12 A,B. Photograph by Dong Lin. Because they were originally used for storage, many Aleut baskets are lidded.

that the decorative pattern shows only on the outside of the basket. Before contact with the whites, Aleut basketmakers sometimes provided color variation in their decorative patterns by dyeing the grass or wrapping it with moose hair, strips of seal gut, or dark brown whale baleen cut from the flexible food-straining material found in the mouths of nontoothed whales. Later basketmakers wrapped grass strands with colored silk thread or embroidery yarn they had procured from white traders.

Traditional Aleutian basket forms were simple and straightforward, typically round or bowl-shaped. Their weaving was far from simple, however, employing the tightest structures achieved by any American basketmakers, sometimes with over forty stitches per inch. By working colored strands into the weave structure, Aleut basketmakers could create delicate designs that were as subtle as the weaving itself. Most designs were patterns of triangles, squares, or diamonds repeated across the basket form. Some artisans added embroidered designs after they wove the basket. Feathers, down, moose hair, bits of seal intestine, or sealskin were also sometimes added as decoration. All of these accents might also be dyed to add color to the monochrome tan of the woven ryegrass.

The arrival of foreigners provided island basketmakers with a commercial outlet for their work. Aleuts began to trade their wares quite early in the nineteenth century as whites eagerly sought souvenirs of the region. Basketmakers quickly expanded their basic vocabulary of forms to accommodate foreign tastes; some even added such novelties as cigar and cigarette cases and lidded bottles to their repertory. Outside sources also influenced and helped vary later designs; some nineteenth-century basket decorations were apparently based on floral embroidery patterns adapted from Russian and European models, while one twentieth-century basketmaker admitted with amusement that some of her designs were taken from a Whitman's Sampler chocolate box—itself an imitation of embroidery.[4]

Traders and tourists also influenced the materials used in the baskets. In addition to the silk thread and yarn these visitors brought to the islands in the nineteenth century, they also eventually exposed Aleut basketmakers to raffia, a fiber derived from the leaf stalks of a Madagascar palm, which many twentieth-century artisans adopted as a ready-made substitute for ryegrass. Although raffia can be woven very tightly, it is coarser than grass, and Aleut baskets made with raffia lack the distinctive and subtle complexity of older, traditional examples.

World War II effectively put an end to the Aleut basketmaking tradition. The Japanese invaded the outer islands of the far-reaching chain in the early years of conflict, taking many Aleutian men prisoner and forcing them to work in their coal mines. Attu Island, the center of Aleut basketmaking and home of its finest craftspeople, was entirely evacuated and never resettled. While the Aleuts ultimately survived the disruption, as had countless others imposed by foreigners, many aspects of their traditional culture, including basketry, did not. Today, the extraordinary baskets woven by earlier Aleut artisans continue to draw attention to this still resilient and resourceful Native American society.

above and left: TWINED BASKETS WITH LIDS

Aleut. Left basket by Anesia Hodikoff, 1934. Others, early 1900s. Aleutian Islands. Rye grass stems (foundation and weft), silk embroidery yarn (design). Diameter of lower right basket: 10 cm, H: 12 cm. California Academy of Sciences, San Francisco; catalog #375 A,B (lower right), #129-13 A,B (above), #129-6 A,B (lower left). Photograph by Dong Lin.

These little trinket baskets were probably made for the tourist trade.

The Pacific Northwest

A painted ceremonial hat, decorated with clan symbols and worn on special occasions such as potlatches. Collector Emma Shaw Colcleugh, a Rhode Island journalist who traveled frequently among the Pacific Northwest Indians, called it "a very valuable specimen."

This twined workbasket is decorated with false embroidery. The Chilkat blanket in the background is typical of those woven by Tlingit wives from goat's wool and cedar bark fibers. The blankets were highly prized by wealthy Tlingit husbands, who commissioned and paid for their creation and also sketched the stylized clan designs with which they were decorated.

The Pacific Northwest was home to one of the most remarkable native cultures in the world. Living along hundreds of miles of rugged coastline, stretching from the mouth of the Columbia River through present-day Washington State and British Columbia and

above: BASKET-COVERED BOTTLE
Tlingit. Collected by Emma Shaw Colcleugh in 1884 or 1885. Wrangell, Alaska. Spruce root, beargrass, maidenhair fern woven over glass bottle. H: 10". Haffenreffer Museum of Anthropology, Brown University, Bristol, Rhode Island.

Northwest coast Indian basketmakers made novelties like this for sale or trade to late Victorian-era tourists. The basket was woven over a "found" mold that could not be removed, creating a craft souvenir that was the opposite of a ship-in-a-bottle.

into southwestern Alaska, the Tlingit, Kwakiutl, Haida, Nootka, Salish, Chinook, and other tribes inhabited a world of almost overwhelming abundance, dominated by prodigious annual runs of salmon returning from the sea to spawn. The region is warmed by the Japan Current, which keeps temperatures moderate year-round and guarantees a rainfall of 80 to 200 inches a year, which supports a multitude of flora and fauna. Watered by the almost constant moisture, the lush and extensive forests surrounding the coast were full of huge Douglas fir, redwood, cedar, and other evergreens. These provided raw material for a wide range of utilitarian objects made by the region's Indians, including their plank homes, enormous dugout sea canoes—some more than 50 feet long—decoratively carved storage chests, baskets, and even clothing, which was woven from bark.

Alone among highly complex and sophisticated Native American societies, the Indians of the northwest coast did not depend on agriculture but rather drew their living almost entirely from the waters of the region. They lived in permanent seaside villages with populations of fifty to three hundred. Salmon, halibut, cod, trout, and other fish, as well as sea otters, whales, seals, and porpoises were so abundant that a few months of summer hunting and fishing supplied enough food for the entire year. This unusual bounty allowed the Indians of the Pacific Northwest to supplement their already considerable wealth by trading with other tribes and with whites. They were also able to organize complex secret societies, to practice lengthy and dramatic rituals of initiation, and to develop a body of ceremonial art unrivaled by any other North American Indian culture.

While best known for their massive heraldic totem poles, fantastic ceremonial masks, intricate shamans' rattles, highly decorated bowls, ladles, and other wood carvings, the Indians of the northwest coast also crafted baskets of extremely high quality. Northwest coast baskets were made primarily from split strips of spruce root and cedar bark, which were tightly twined or plaited. Like those of the Aleuts, northwest coast Indian baskets, particularly those of the Tlingit, were often decorated with false embroidery. The Haida and Tlingit were both prolific basketmakers who created baskets with similar heraldic designs, but the Haida did not employ false embroidery. Decorative patterns in Haida and Tlingit basketry typically consisted of bands or patterns of triangles, crosses, diamonds, or zigzag lines often executed in bold red and black. As inveterate and resourceful

traders, the Indians of the northwest coast quickly incorporated
aniline dyes into their work,
eschewing natural dyes in favor of
the brighter chemical colors soon
after their introduction into the
region in the late 1860s.

The most common northwest
coast basket form was a simple
open cylinder made in a variety of
sizes and used for gathering and
storing berries and other foods.
Wild berries were among the few
plant foods available to the
region's Indians, whose diet consisted primarily of fish, animal
protein, and fat.

Many northwestern tribes
made basketry hats. Some of these
were bowl-shaped utilitarian rain
hats, so tightly woven that they
shed water. Northwest coast
Indians often went without
clothes in good weather, but
when the rains came, they wore
loose-fitting waterproof capes
woven from cedar bark, and hats
made from spruce roots. The
Tlingit, Haida, and Kwakiutl also

above: SKOKOMISH CHIEF'S
DAUGHTER with baskets, Puget
Sound region, Washington, c. 1915.
Photograph by Edward Sheriff Curtis.

made wide-brimmed ceremonial hats, which they decorated with painted
clan markings and wore as symbols of status. These distinctively decorated
hats were usually woven by women and painted by men. The Nootka tribe
produced onion-domed hats decorated with realistic depictions of whale
hunting, which were probably clan symbols as well as records of actual
hunting experiences. The explorers Captain James Cook and Meriwether
Lewis, of the Lewis and Clark expedition, both collected hats like this

during their trips to the region in 1778–1779 and 1805–1806. Those hats are now in the Peabody Museum at Harvard.

Woven rattle-lid baskets were also unique to the Northwest. These small, round storage containers had hollow-centered lids that held pebbles, lead shot, seeds, or small round stones taken from the gizzards of birds. The loose objects inside the lid rattled whenever the baskets were moved or opened. These ingenious baskets were often presented as gifts and became particularly popular with late nineteenth-century collectors, who used them as trinket containers. Many were specifically produced for sale to whites as novelties rather than for use by Indians.

Northwest coast tribes were unique among American Indians in their obsession with rank, status, and the accumulation and display of material wealth, characteristics they shared with the whites. Northwest coast societies were organized into ancestral clans that lived communally in large multifamily dwellings. These clans were rigidly hierarchical and highly class conscious. Every member of a tribe held a different and carefully calibrated rank, which reflected his or her hereditary status, personal achievements, and wealth. Indians competed fiercely with each other for rank and could move up or down the social ladder, depending on their success.

Gift-giving was crucial to the social life of northwest coast Indians. They believed that the natural bounty which surrounded them was a gift that had to be acknowledged in order to keep the natural cycle in motion. They ceremonially welcomed the first salmon caught each year, for example, and returned to the sea the bones of all the salmon they caught, thereby ensuring a plentiful catch the next year. The same principle extended to their social order. Even more important than gathering wealth was giving it away as a display of wealth and status: the more one gave away, the richer one was seen to be. The potlatch, a winter ceremonial feast unique to the region, was the central social and spiritual event in most northwest coast communities. Potlatches were ostensibly held to celebrate a marriage, a death, a change in rank, or the completion of a new clan house. But, more important, they allowed hosts to display their wealth and status by lavishly sharing with others. Hosts began to prepare for a potlatch a year or more in advance by stockpiling supplies and gifts, including baskets, blankets, and carvings, in fantastic quantities. They needed to provide vast amounts of food and drink for their gluttonous guests, who could number in the hun-

opposite: CHIEF'S HAT

Nootka. Early nineteenth century. Puget Sound region. Twined cedar bark. Peabody Museum of Archaeology and Ethnology, Harvard University, Cambridge, Massachusetts. Photograph by Hillel Burger.

A companion to this early onion-domed hat, also in the Peabody Museum collection, was collected by Lewis and Clark during their winter stay at the mouth of the Columbia in 1805–1806. Whale hunting was central to the Nootka and Makah, who hunted the leviathans from massive dugout sea canoes. Their harpoons were attached to lengthy rope lines dotted with air-filled sealskin floats.

following pages: BABY BASKET

Lillooet. c. 1900. Washington. Cedar bark and roots, wool, glass beads, buckskin, wood. H: 4½", L: 25¼", W: 12". Lauren Rogers Museum of Art, Laurel, Mississippi. Gift of Catherine Marshall Gardiner.

The wooden arch of this carrier supported a protective head covering, the baby was strapped in place with the lacing buckskin flaps. The basket's cedar bark carrying strap could be looped across the mother's forehead or chest.

dreds and stay as long as twelve days. Both hosts and guests performed costumed songs and dramas traditional to their clan, and the hosts dispensed gift after gift to their guests, each carefully considered and appropriate to the recipient's station. In the eyes of both hosts and guests, profligacy in this context was the truest measure of honor and wealth.[5]

Indians of the southern Puget Sound region, such as the Quinault and Skokomish, specialized in soft, collapsible baskets, which they used to gather clams, berries, and other dietary staples. Their gathering baskets were twined from spruce root, and a number of spruce root loops often encircled the rims. Both tribes also made distinctive flat-twined wallets from split cattail reeds. Across the Cascade Mountains to the west, in present-day Washington and Oregon, plateau tribes such as the Cayuse, Wasco, and Nez Percé also wove flat wallets, which they used as saddlebags. Unlike the coastal Indians who traveled by water, the members of these tribes were superb horsemen. Plateau Indians twined their wallets from hemp, which grew wild in the region, and they originally decorated them with colored reeds or bear grass. In the late nineteenth century, dyed corn husks became the most popular decorative material for plateau basketry wallets, which have come to be known as corn husk bags. During the early years of the twentieth century, however, beads supplanted corn husks. Whether using husks or beads, plateau basketmakers decorated each side of the bag with a different geometric or stylized floral design. When aniline dyes were adopted early in the twentieth century, the wide range of color allowed artisans to develop pictorial designs that included everything from birds and animals to American flags.

left: GATHERING BASKET

Quinault or Skokomish. Nineteenth century. Collected in the Quinault village of Taholah, Washington. Twined spruce root and bear grass, spruce root loops. H: 25.4 cm. National Museum of the American Indian, Smithsonian.

Puget Sound Indians such as the Quinault and Skokomish traded frequently with the Nez Percé and other Cascades tribes and were influenced by their style of twined basketry as well as by that of other coastal basketmakers in the Northwest. Puget Sound artisans often finished their twined baskets with loops of twisted spruce root or cedar bark.

opposite: FOOD BASKET

Haida. Collected by Emma Shaw Colcleugh c. 1885. Queen Charlotte Islands, British Columbia. Spruce root, beargrass, maidenhair fern. H: 10", D: 10". Haffenreffer Museum of Anthropology, Brown University, Bristol, Rhode Island. Photograph by Cathy Carver.

Tightly woven baskets like this were used by northwest coast Indians to carry water and cook foods. Food was cooked by dropping red hot stones into water or meal mush.

following pages: PLATEAU CORN HUSK BAG

Possibly Nez Percé. c. 1890. Eastern Washington. Twined hemp, dyed corn husks, yarn, rawhide, beads. 12" x 10". Collection of Allan Lobb. Photographs by Art Wolfe.

As is typical of twined Plateau bags, this example carries entirely different decorations on its opposing sides. When used as a saddlebag, only one side would be visible at a time.

California and the Great Basin

The native peoples of California and the adjoining Great Basin of present-day Utah and Nevada made some of the finest baskets in the Native American world. Unlike the tribes of the Southwest, these Indians did not make pottery, so baskets served

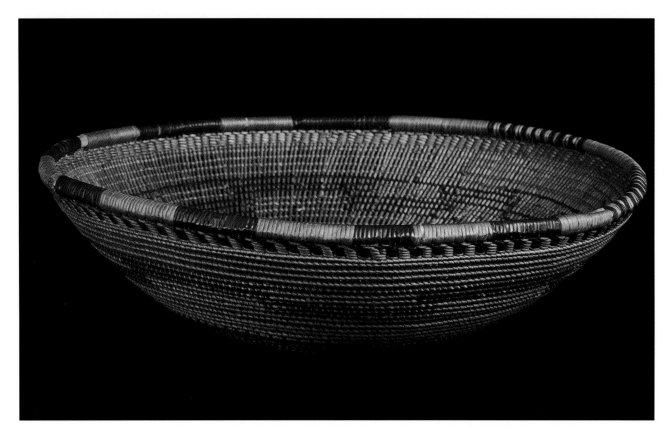

above: BASKET TRAY

Pomo. c. early 1900s. Central California. Twined willow shoots (foundation), willow and redbud shoots (weft). H: 13.3 cm, D: 44.4 cm. California Academy of Sciences, San Francisco. Elkus Collection. Catalog #370-898. Photograph by Dong Lin.

A fine example of a utilitarian Pomo basket, most likely woven by a man. Baskets of this type were used to sift acorn meal, to parch seeds, and to serve food.

many purposes in their daily life. Baskets also provided the women of the California and Great Basin tribes with their primary creative outlet. Such tribes as the Washo and Pomo created extraordinary baskets of unparalleled quality and imaginative power. The basket masterpieces of this area were among the first collected and appreciated for their artistry by anthropologists, historians, and collectors of Native American arts, and they remain among the crowning achievements of world basketry.

Although California's Indians were foragers, hunters, and gatherers, they were not nomadic: the region's rich natural resources supported small permanent settlements. The Pomo and other northern tribes occupied a land of plenty where the rivers were full of migratory salmon and other fish and the forests abounded with game, including deer, rabbits, and ducks, and a variety of berries, nuts, tubers, and wild vegetables. The climate was moderate most of the year, and ample rainfall provided a reliable supply of water. Tribes living along the coast could depend on many types of saltwater fish and shellfish, including yellowtails, tuna, oysters, clams, and

mussels. The meaty foot of the abalone provided a delicious steak, but the giant shellfish was equally prized for its lustrous shell, which could be cut into small pieces to make jewelry or to decorate baskets.

Although California's Indians crafted remarkable baskets for many centuries, historians have long agreed that the Pomo, who lived north of San Francisco Bay, created the most sophisticated and creative American baskets. Pomo work ranged in size from functional baskets three feet in diameter to miniatures so tiny that several can fit on a dime. In contrast to the practices of most other tribes, basketmaking was not exclusively women's work among the Pomo. Both men and women made baskets, with men crafting utilitarian baskets and women concentrating on the more difficult and time-consuming decorative and ceremonial pieces. The Pomo were masters of both twining and coiling; no other tribe employed both techniques, and only the Pomo used four different twining techniques. Some of their baskets were so tightly woven that they held water and were used to boil acorn mush. Acorns, a staple in the diet of most

above: UTILITY BASKET BOWL
Yokuts. c. 1900. Tule River, Tulare County, California. Coiled grass sewn with white slough root, willow bark and (probably) devil's claw. H: 7¾" D: 18¼". Lauren Rogers Museum of Art, Laurel, Mississippi. Gift of Catherine Marshall Gardiner.
Flare-sided bowls like this were a specialty of Yokuts coilers. The decorative bands of triangles were probably intended to imitate the markings of the diamondback rattlesnake.

This assemblage offers a variety of Pomo decorative techniques. In addition to quail topknot feathers, Pomo artisans often attached pendants of sparkling seed beads and iridescent abalone shells to the sides and rims of their gift baskets or encircled the rims with flat shell beads. The small glass-beaded basket at the center is decorated in a simple geometric pattern, while the strong diagonal designs on the basket at far right are dotted with pieces of glittering shell beads.

California Indians, were pounded into meal and blanched in hot water to remove the bitter taste of tannic acid. The resulting acid-free meal could then be either boiled into a bland mush by dropping hot stones into the mixture or used as flour for unleavened bread.

The Pomo are also rightly renowned for the unique decorative embellishments they added to some of their baskets, including feathers, glass, clamshell beads, pieces of magnesite, and carved abalone shells. The most remarkable Pomo baskets were completely covered with feathers, creating a surface almost as softly inviting and richly colored as a bird's breast. Red feathers were plucked from the crests of woodpeckers, and green ones from the necks and heads of mallard ducks, while other bright-colored feathers came from orioles, bluebirds, meadowlarks, and even hummingbirds. Rim decorations often included the black topknots of quail. Pomo women made their feathered baskets as ceremonial gifts for important people or to celebrate special dates. They were sometimes given to girls to mark life passages such as birth, puberty, and marriage and were

so treasured by the recipients that they were often cremated with a deceased owner. Remarkably, women also sometimes used these elaborate baskets for cooking or gathering food.

Other outstanding California Indian basketmakers include the Maidu, Klamath, Karok, and Hupa in the northern part of the state and the Yokuts and Chumash in the south. The Yokuts and Chumash, whose coiled basketry was influenced by nearby southwestern traditions, created especially fine lidded jar-shaped treasure baskets with wide flared shoulders. Southern California coilers, who worked primarily with bunched grasses, excelled in crafting globular forms with exaggerated flaring sides. Basketmakers commonly incorporated juncus (*Juncus textiles*) in their basketry. This locally abundant rush created a distinctive mottled gold surface.

The nomadic way of life of Great Basin Indians remained unchanged for many centuries. Historians believe that before the arrival of the whites, California supported a quarter million Indians of dozens of different tribes, but the 200,000 square miles of the Great Basin were home to only

above: MONO HOME WITH
BASKETS, east central California,
c. 1925. Curtis commented: "The wickiup shown is a typical winter shelter, and
the utensils are burden-baskets and
winnowing-trays. All these baskets were
appurtenances of the one wickiup."
Photograph by Edward Sheriff Curtis.

a handful of widely scattered tribes, including the Washo, Mono, and
Panamint. Living in small, autonomous, self-sustaining family groups,
Great Basin Indians wandered constantly throughout their desert homeland in search of food, water, and firewood. Their staple foods included
jackrabbits, lizards, cactus fruits, seeds, insects, pine nuts, and desert rats.
Clothing and shelter were equally basic and meager, due to the sweltering
climate and the scarcity of raw materials. Jackrabbit-skin robes provided
warmth during the winter, and the nomads built crude cone-shaped shel-
ters of willow poles covered with bundles of reeds and open at the top.
They abandoned these temporary huts whenever the search for food
required a move.

Well-made lightweight utilitarian baskets were essential to the wan-
dering lifestyle of the Great Basin Indians, who hoarded food and water in

order to survive. Basketmakers fashioned burden baskets, water jars, seed beaters, winnowing trays, cradles, and bowls. Basketmaking traditions in the region are traceable back at least nine thousand years through archaeological evidence provided by carbon-dating baskets preserved by the arid climate. One of the most interesting archaeological discoveries from the region is a group of realistic canvasback duck decoys fashioned from reeds and feathers, and found in a cave in Nevada in the 1920s. These basketry birds, which are at least a thousand years old and may date to as much as a millennium earlier, establish the American Indian as the inventor of the decoy, an indigenous American folk art that was to be copied and perfected by European immigrants in the nineteenth century.

In contrast to the diversity of approaches taken by California's basketmakers, the Great Basin Indians primarily coiled their baskets. The Paiute, Panamint, and especially the Washo, who lived near Lake Tahoe, all made coiled baskets of exceptional quality. Willow (*Salit* sp.) and sumac (*Rhus* sp.), which grew near water holes and streambeds, were the most common materials and were used both for foundations and stitches. One of the most common decorative materials was devil's-claw (*Martiynia probosidea*), a desert plant that provided a natural black fiber. Great Basin basketmakers created simple geometric designs with devil's-claw, which contrasted against the light-colored willow and sumac.

In the last years of the nineteenth century, Indian baskets became extremely popular with the American public who perceived them as relics of a conquered and dying culture, a vanishing race. Selling for only a few dollars apiece, they held an honored place amid the bric-a-brac in the late Victorian home. A number of museum curators and serious collectors also became interested in Indian baskets, recognizing them as an important Native American art form. The decades between the Centennial and the start of World War I were a great age for both museum building and ethnology in America, and many major natural history museums financed field expeditions that gathered Native American artifacts from tribes and traders throughout the country.

Dealers and trading posts played an important part in the early

below: BASKETRY DUCK DECOYS
Unknown Native American artist. c. A.D. 200. Humboldt County, Nevada. Tule reeds, duck feathers. natural pigments. L: 26.5, 27 cm. National Museum of the American Indian, Smithsonian. These ancient basketry decoys were made to imitate canvasbacks, the king of American game ducks. The painted and feathered bird represents a drake, while the plain reed bird may either be unfinished or intended to represent the drably colored hen of the species.

right: CHEMEHUEVIS BASKET-
MAKER posing with some of her work.
Southern California or Nevada, c. 1900.
Chemehuevis basketry shows influence
of both Great Basin and Southwest coil-
ing styles.
Courtesy Museum of New Mexico; photo
#82624.

opposite: BOTTLENECK BASKET
Panamint. c. 1900. Death Valley region, California.
Willow, devil's claw, yucca root, white quills. H: 5";
diameter at shoulder: 7⅝". Lauren Rogers Museum
of Art, Laurel, Mississippi. Gift of Catherine
Marshall Gardiner.
This form, called a seed jar, bottleneck
or treasure basket, was made by several
southern California tribes, including the
Panamint and Yokuts. This example
alternates two decorative panels, one
depicting a lizard, men, and a deer, the
other a triangular pattern that probably
represents a diamondback rattlesnake.

below: COOKING BASKET
Mary Benson. c. 1900–1950. Central California.
Twined sedge, redbud and willow. H: 24 cm.
National Museum of the American Indian,
Smithsonian.
Although this example was made for sale
to a collector, the Pomo traditionally
used watertight baskets of this form to
cook acorn mush.

twentieth-century revival of Native
American basketry, which centered on
the highest quality California and
Great Basin baskets. Abram Cohn,
for example, was a Carson City,
Nevada, entrepreneur and trading
post owner who encouraged and
promoted the work of a remarkable Washo basketmaker he dubbed
Datsolalee and whose given name
was Louisa Keyser. (Cohn's nickname translates as "fat-in-the-hips."
Although his protégée was a substantial
woman, Cohn's disparaging nickname is
more suggestive of the bigotry and sexism of
whites at the time.) Keyser's baskets grew out of the highly sophisticated
and technically accomplished Washo tradition, but were self-conscious
works of art, made specifically for sale to collectors and museums rather
than for her own use. Some experts consider Keyser, who died in 1925, the
greatest basketmaker of all time. The globular forms of her coiled willow,
rosebud, and fern-root bowls, which she called degikups, reflected the
Pomo's treasure baskets and employ as many as thirty stitches to the inch.
One of her works—a 16½-inch-diameter basket that took over a year to
complete—contains an estimated 100,000 stitches, and several others con-
tain well over half of that number.

Through Cohn's efforts, Keyser received nationwide
acclaim, and her baskets brought phenomenal prices for the
time. The influential collector George Wharton James
declared Keyser's work "exquisite" and reported that "her
baskets have brought . . . prices ranging from $150 to
$250. Three of her recent baskets are valued even higher.
[Her] work is wonderful in its shape, symbolization, and
weave. [Her] delicacy of touch, artistic skill, and poetical
conception excite admiration."[6]
Keyser was the central figure in the commercial and aesthetic revival of Great Basin basketry, and the degikup form she

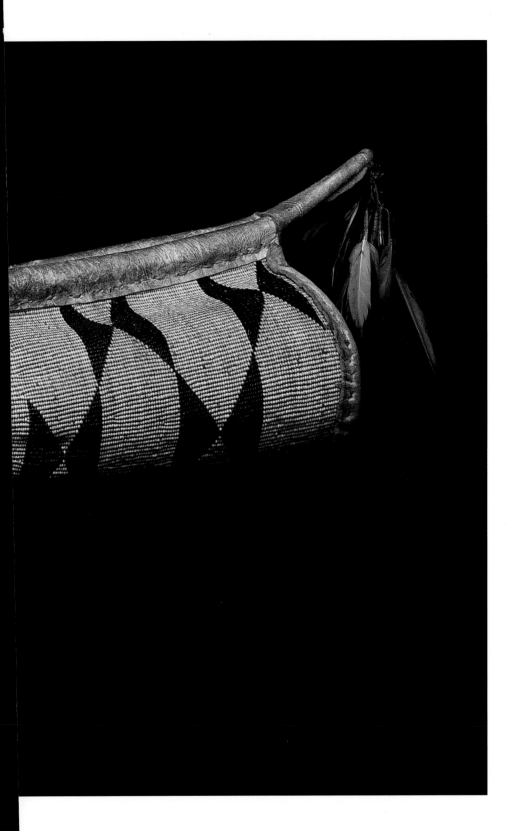

left: JUMPING DANCE BASKET
Karok (attributed). Late nineteenth century.
Northern California. Willow, conifer root, beargrass,
maidenhair fern, feathers, deerskin. Southwest
Museum, Los Angeles. Photograph by Don Meyer.
The ceremonial jumping dance was performed by men of several northern
California tribes, who wore headbands
decorated with red feathers plucked from
the scalps of Acorn woodpeckers and
who tied tubular baskets like this around
their waists. The oddly shaped ceremonial
baskets were intended to represent the
elkhorn purses in which Indians kept
dentalium shell money. Stuffed with grass
to retain their shape, the bulging oversized purses symbolized great wealth.

following page: GIFT BASKET
Pomo. Nineteenth century. Central California.
Sedge root, willow, woodpecker and quail top knot
feathers, clam and abalone shells, cotton twine. H:
3¼", D: 13½". The Southwest Museum, Los
Angeles.
The earliest Pomo gift baskets were decorated with red feathers plucked from
the crown of the locally common Acorn
woodpecker and were intended to hang
by a cord strung with shiny bits of shell.

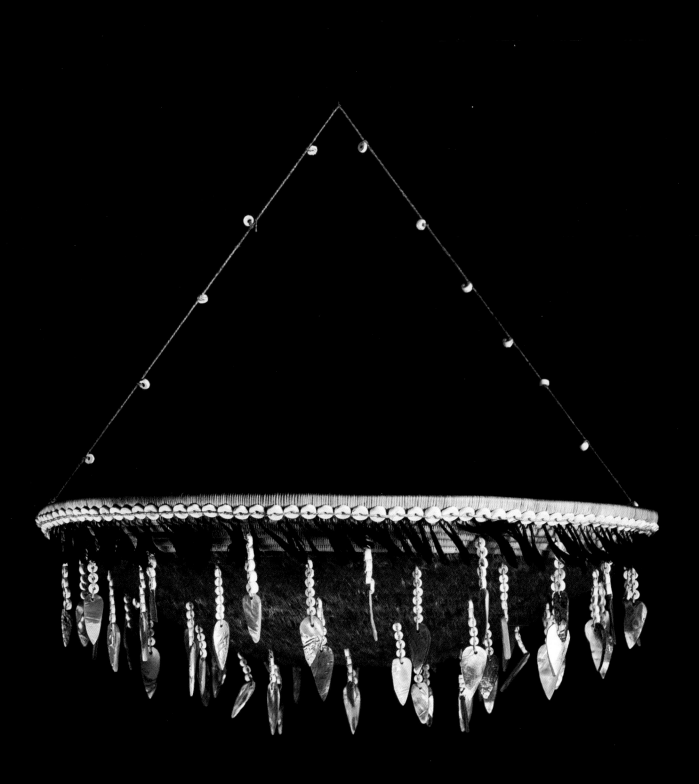

Collecting

BASKETS by California and Great Basin Indians were among the first to be sought by collectors, and they remain the most highly regarded and consistently valuable of all American baskets. George Wharton James proclaimed that their makers "displayed exquisite taste in shape, consummate skill in weave, artistic conception in ornamentation, and . . . an appreciation of the harmony of colors few Americans can surpass."[7] Many collectors feel that such treasures as feather-covered Pomo "jewel" baskets, Yurok and Panamint bottle-necked jars, and Great Basin degikups represent the pinnacle of the basketmaker's art, and prime examples can bring fierce competition and premium prices. As they were in their own time, the rare and remarkable baskets of Louisa Keyser continue to be popular. A fine example of Keyser's work is still the ultimate prize for many collectors of Indian baskets.

As with other high-priced antiques, provenance can have a major influence on the value of a basket. Having been part of an early or highly respected private collection can increase a basket's value significantly. A well-documented provenance often strengthens collectors' confidence in the integrity and importance of a particular basket or group of baskets and can help assure the buyer that his or her investment is secure. Many large and remarkable collections of baskets and other Native American artifacts were acquired between 1880 and 1940.

In a 1902 report issued by the Smithsonian Institution, basket scholar Otis Tufton Mason said he knew of more than one hundred significant private collections of baskets. These early collectors often had the enormous advantage of dealing directly with Indian artisans or family members. Early collections from the United States, Canada, and Great Britain, where a surprising number of American Indian artifacts were gathered during the Victorian age, occasionally become available through major dealers and auction houses.

above: LOUISA KEYSER (A.K.A. DATSOLALEE), legendary Washo basketmaker, posing with some of her work, 1897.
Nevada State Museum, Carson City, Nevada.

DEGIKUP
Louisa Keyser (Washo). 1917–1918. Carson City, Nevada. Willow, bracken fern, redbud. H: 12", D: 16¼". Philbrook Museum of Art, Tulsa, Oklahoma, Clark Field Collection.
Keyser's degikups are among the most tightly sewn coiled baskets ever made. This masterpiece of the basketmaker's art has thirty stitches per inch.

right: GATHERING BASKET

Maidu. c. early 1900s. Central California. Coiled willow shoots sewn with split redbud shoots. H: 74 cm, D: 113 cm. California Academy of Sciences, San Francisco. Catalog #136-2. Photograph by Dong Lin.

This immense open-mouthed basket was probably used in gathering seeds. Maidu artisans often decorated their coiled baskets with simple geometric designs, in this case using reddish-brown redbud to contrast against the tan ground of willow.

opposite: COVERED FANCY BASKET

Elizabeth Conrad Hickox (Wiyot/Karok). c. 1920. Klamath River area, northwestern California. Twined hazel shoots, beargrass, maidenhair fern, and dyed porcupine quills. H: 7¼", D: 5½". Lauren Rogers Museum of Art, Laurel, Mississippi. Gift of Catherine Marshall Gardiner.

This typically masterful example of Hickox's work is woven with seventeen stitches per inch. She created the decorative pattern by combining false-embroidered dark brown maidenhair fern stems with porcupine quills that had been dyed yellow with oak tree lichen. Indians dried dull white and tan porcupine quills before dyeing them. Women chewed the three-to-five-inch-long quills to soften them, then flattened and wove them into place with a needle. Quills were far more commonly used to decorate leather clothing, moccasins, and pouches than baskets, and their use was an anacronism by Hickox's time.

below right: BABY RATTLE

Kathy Wallace. 1994. Fairfield, California. Spruce root, willow shoots, woodwardia fern dyed with white alder bark and bear grass, handle wrapped with willow root. L: 7", W: 2". Photograph by Janet Caron-Owens, courtesy California Indian Basketweavers Association, Nevada City, California.

invented was imitated by many of her contemporaries, including Tootsie Dick Sam, whose work Abram Cohn also championed. Another well-known professional basketmaker was Elizabeth Conrad Hickox (1873– 1947), the daughter of a German father and a Wiyot Indian mother, who created diminutive knobbed fancy baskets decorated with traditional designs, which she worked with the stems of black maidenhair ferns. Hickox worked for many years under contract to a Pasadena art dealer and collector named Grace Nicholson, who promoted her work widely; virtually every major natural history museum collection in the country includes her baskets, which are instantly recognizable. Nicholson also represented the masterful Pomo basketmaker Mary Benson (1876–1950), who, like Hickox, wrought subtle variations on traditional tribal themes.

The new market for Indian baskets inevitably influenced basket forms and techniques. Ironically, the artisans produced some of the finest traditional-style Indian baskets for sale to whites, whose encroachments had forever altered the traditions themselves. Indian basketmakers seized the economic opportunity presented by tourists and collectors, however, and changed their products to suit the tastes of their clientele. The baskets of Louisa Keyser, Mary Benson, Elizabeth Hickox, and other Revival-era masters are personal, artistic refinements of traditional forms, designed specifically to appeal to the white collectors with whom the basketmakers and their agents interacted. Similarly, early twentieth-century Pomo basketmakers expanded the range of decoration on their baskets in response to requests from collectors, creating works with banded patterns of multicolored feathers where previously only two or three colors had been used.

above, left: WUKCHUMNI ARTISAN JENNIFER MALONE showing off a twined basket "spider" start she learned in Holly Henscher's twining class at the California Indian Basketweavers Association Gathering, Thousand Oaks, California, June 1997.
Photograph by Linda Yamane, courtesy CIBA.

above, center: MOUNTAIN MAIDU BASKETMAKER DENISE DAVIS working on a peeled willow burden basket at the California Indian Basketweavers Association Gathering, Thousand Oaks, California, June 1997. Although Davis's grandmothers and "aunties" were well-known basketmakers, her mother, like most Indians of her generation, did not choose to weave, and Davis herself did not begin making baskets until after her children were grown. Her mentor has been Maidu master basketweaver Lily Baker, who was born in 1911.
Photograph by Dugin Aguilar, courtesy CIBA.

above, right: WESTERN MONO BASKETMAKER JULIE TEX teaching at the California Indian Basketweavers Association Gathering, Thousand Oaks, California, June 1997.
Photograph by Robert Dorame, courtesy CIBA.

Today many of the ancient basketmaking traditions of California and the Great Basin are endangered. In many Indian communities, few tribal elders remain to pass their knowledge on to new generations, and most young people have little interest in learning the time-consuming handcrafts of their ancestors. Enough craftspeople remain to keep the traditions alive for the time being, but the intrusion of America's homogenizing mainstream culture continues to undermine the integrity and durability of the old ways.

Basketmaking has been bolstered in recent years by the efforts of the California Indian Basketweavers Association, a nonprofit advocacy group centered in Nevada City, California, whose mission is "to preserve, promote and perpetuate California Indian basketweaving traditions." Founded in 1992, the CIBA now has over 600 members, 200 of whom are Native American artisans. The association has helped to create a new community of California Indian basketmakers, linking formerly isolated craftspeople from across the state and serving as a central information exchange. CIBA publishes an illustrated quarterly newsletter; sponsors an annual gathering for basketmakers and their guests; provides classes and lectures for Indian children and the general public; and lobbies legislators on a wide range of issues.

Since basketmakers depend on wild plants for their materials, protection and proper management of the many different plants they use is a major issue for the CIBA. Most Indians gather basketmaking materials on public lands, where the use of herbicides can threaten the health and safety of plants and gatherers alike. As basketmaker Dee Dominguez pointed out at a symposium at the Southwest Museum, "We put these plants in our mouths and in our hands. We have to have a healthy plant to have a healthy basket."[8] The CIBA has served as a powerful group voice for change in land-management practices in cooperation with such agencies as the EPA, the U.S. Forest Service, and the Department of the Interior, all of which are learning to take the needs of Native American basketmakers into consideration. In an interview, CIBA founder and president Sara Greensfelder has noted that "As word gets out about the organization, basketweavers are being asked to address conferences as spokespeople for traditional Indian culture and traditional Indian land-management practices. People are starting to recognize that Native people were land managers for thousands of years and they're good at it."[9]

Not everyone is enthusiastic about promoting the art and tradition of basketmaking, however. In 1997 Republican congressman Wally Herger of California sent every House member a copy of a $60,500 grant notice to CIBA from the National Endowment for the Arts, along with his note: "This grant announcement for basketweavers is a prime example of why the NEA should be eliminated." After howls of protest from insulted basketmakers, congressional defenses by NEA chair Jane Alexander and Colorado Senator Ben Nighthorse Campbell, and a wave of California newspaper editorials supporting the grant, a Herger spokesman explained that the congressman thinks "basketweaving is a wonderful pastime . . . and it's probably a better use of time than television, but we just don't see where there's a justification to ask the taxpayer to fund this hobby."[10]

CIBA is helping to educate many others about the significance of California's basket-making traditions. The association has served as a model for new regional organizations of Indian basketmakers, including groups in Maine, the Pacific Northwest, the Great Lakes, and the Great Basin. Perhaps organizations like CIBA represent the best chance for the survival of traditional Indian basketmaking, as Native Americans rediscover the value of their artistic and cultural roots and learn the power of solidarity.

below: ACORN SIFTER
Denise Davis (Mountain Maidu). 1993. Chico, California. Winter and spring redbud, willow. D: 11". Photograph by Janet Caron-Owens, courtesy California Indian Basketweavers Association, Nevada City, California.
The logo of the California Indian Basketweavers Association is based on this example of Davis's work. This type of three-rod coil basket was traditionally used to sift acorn flour. Winter redbud provides the color in the geometric design.

The Southwest

The American Southwest—comprising Arizona, New Mexico, and southern Colorado and Utah—is a land of spectacular natural beauty. Vast barren deserts, towering forest-covered mountains, deep river-cut canyons, oddly shaped buttes, and

above: HAVASUPAI BASKETMAKER outside her home in Cataract Canyon, Arizona, c. 1912.

Photograph by Willard J. Chamberlain.

steep, flat-topped mesas distinguish the region's unique and dramatic landscape. The climate is harsh, dry, and often extreme: scorching sun-baked days can be followed by chilling nights. Sagebrush, mesquite, prickly pear, and saguaro cactus are among the distinctive plants of the desert lowlands, with piñon pine, juniper, and yellow pine dominating higher elevations.

The Native American cultures of the Southwest are ancient, with lineages that stretch beyond recorded history. Two of the three major early cultures of the region, the Hohokam, who lived in present-day southern Arizona, and the Anasazi, who occupied the Four Corners region where Arizona, New Mexico, Utah, and Colorado meet, were peaceful and sophisticated farmers who grew corn and other sun-loving crops in irrigated desert fields. The most familiar of the Southwest's early people are the Anasazi, whose descendants were called Pueblos by the Spanish, for the attached adobe homes in which they lived. The astonishing clifftop ruins of Mesa Verde in Colorado, where eight hundred years ago as many as 7,000 Indians may have dwelt, are one of many surviving Anasazi-built pueblos.

The Native American cultures of the Southwest were the least changed by contact with whites of any in North America. The region saw its share of conflict, from savage encounters with early Spanish adventurers such as Coronado in the mid-1500s to battles with U.S. government forces in the late nineteenth century. However, because the largely desert land was poor and much of it undesirable to white settlers and developers, many of the region's Indians were able to live undisturbed where they had for centuries. The largest tracts of U.S. land still owned by Indians are in

Anasazi. c. 1100–1300. Southern Utah. Natural and dyed sumac. Largest diameter: 11½". The Southwest Museum, Los Angeles.

The Anasazi, also known as the Basketmakers for the many woven and coiled bowls and trays they left behind, are believed to be the ancestors of the Hopi and other modern Pueblo Indians. These ancient coiled baskets demonstrate how sophisticated their art was.

northeastern Arizona and northwestern New Mexico, and the oldest continuously occupied settlement in North America is the pueblo at old Oraibi in Arizona, where the Hopi have lived for nearly a thousand years. While the homogenizing forces of the modern world threaten the survival of their culture, many Hopi still live in much the same way their ancestors did a millennium ago.

Although the native peoples of the Southwest are best known for their extraordinary pottery and weaving traditions, basketmaking has always been an important craft in the region. Some of the earliest documented American baskets were made in the Southwest. Preserved in large numbers by the desert climate, these ancient baskets were made by the early, pre–pueblo building Anasazi, who prospered from the beginning of the Christian era to about A.D. 700. The well-made coiled and stitched baskets produced by the Basketmakers, as they are called by anthropologists, are the most significant artifacts remaining from their culture. The Basketmakers created pieces to serve a wide range of domestic and agri-

cultural purposes, often decorating them with bold geometric designs. Some of their baskets are virtually indistinguishable from pieces made hundreds of years later. Their craftsmanship set a high standard of achievement that has been maintained for centuries by succeeding tribes in the region, including the Hopi, Zuni, Navajo, Havasupai, Papago, Pima, and Western Apache, all of whom produced outstanding baskets.

Like their peers in southern California and the Great Basin, southwest basketmakers were masters of coiling techniques. Coiled baskets were the dominant southwestern type as long ago as 2000 B.C., and flat circular plaques and trays, shallow ceremonial bowls, and bulging urn-shaped storage jars remain closely identified with the region nearly four thousand years later. From early times, these natives practiced two basic types of coiling, using two different kinds of material. Coiled baskets were made either from willowlike rods, or from bundles of grass or other thin plant fibers such as cattail, wheat straw, or yucca. Rods could be coiled individually or arranged in horizontal or vertical groups of two or three. Bundles of plant fiber could be used exclusively, or they could be combined with rods to create a mixed foundation. Whatever the materials, however, the resulting coils were held together with stitching, usually made of willow or cottonwood. The basketmaker proceeded one row, or course, at a time, interlocking adjoining coils by sewing or looping stitching through the preceding coil, or simply looping noninterlocking stitches around both courses. By adding colored material to the stitching, the basketmaker could create patterns and overall designs.

Among the most talented basketmakers of the Southwest, the Pima and Papago of southwest Arizona produced baskets similar to those of the ancient Anasazi basketmakers. Although both the Pima and the Papago made other utilitarian forms, their most notable baskets are highly ornate coiled food bowls and winnowing trays. The coils of these baskets, usually made from bunches of grass or cattails, were tightly sewn with light-colored willow and black splint stripped from the seedpods of devil's-claw, which provided a tough, long-lasting material. With this native desert plant, Pima and Papago craftspeople created a solid black circle at the center of their baskets, from which they extended whirling abstract geometric designs, such as mazes of fretted, stepped lines. A black rim finished and contained the design. The resourcefulness and creativity of nineteenth-

and early twentieth-century Pima and Papago artisans is astonishing; their baskets display seemingly endless variations on traditional themes and motifs.

Among Pueblo peoples, the Hopi have created the best-known baskets; they are so familiar that they represent southwestern basketmaking for many people. The baskets, however, differ from the work of other tribes in the region and have no obvious connections to Anasazi or other early southwestern baskets. The Hopis worked within two equally distinctive methods. Residents of the villages of Second Mesa made coiled baskets, while those of old Oraibi and other Third Mesa villages made plaited wicker baskets. Hopi coiled baskets are distinguished from other southwestern examples by their large bundled coils, which are often an inch or more thick. Artisans fashioned the coils from bunches of galleta grass or shredded yucca and tightly sewed them with yucca-leaf splints. They created Third Mesa wicker baskets by weaving wefts of rabbitbrush over and under warps of sumac.

Although the Hopi also made shallow trays and deep bowls, their most familiar basket form is the flat circular plaque, typically decorated with geometric designs representing rain, clouds, and other natural forces, or with kachinas, the Hopi spirit figures best known in doll form. The Hopi used plaques as ceremonial trays to hold cornmeal, bread, fruit, and dry foods. Plaques also served as wedding gifts; they were made by female friends and relatives of the bride for the groom and his family and carried symbolic meaning. The Hopi's colorful designs, which stand in marked contrast to the stark black-and-white decorative palette of other regional tribes, were created by dyeing the yucca stitching or rabbitbrush weft with a variety of natural plant and mineral pigments. Artisans preferred the brilliant aniline dyes when they were introduced in the 1880s but have used them more sparingly for many years, choosing instead the softer and more harmonious colors produced by natural dyes.

Hopi basket traditions are actively carried on today by a number of residents

above: RIO GRANDE PUEBLO GIRL balancing a basket of threshed grain on her head. San Juan, New Mexico, c. 1925. Southwest Indians often carried loaded baskets or water jars on their heads. They winnowed their grain by pouring it from baskets like this onto cloth spread on the ground. *Photograph by Edward Sheriff Curtis.*

left: COILED BOWL
Hopi. Late nineteenth century. Second Mesa, Arizona. Bundled grass sewn with yucca fiber. Haffenreffer Museum of Anthropology, Brown University, Bristol, Rhode Island.
The decorative designs on this thickly coiled bowl represent cloud terraces and the Hopi ancestral spirits called *kachinas.*

opposite: BASKET TRAYS
Pima. top to bottom: c. 1920–30, 1955, 1946. Arizona. Center: Alice Robertson Collection, University of Tulsa. Top and bottom: Gift of Clark Field, Philbrook Museum of Art, Tulsa, Oklahoma.
Although these examples were probably made for collectors, the Pima traditionally used shallow trays like these for mixing and serving food. The broad flat expanse of the baskets also offered Pima basketmakers an ideal canvas for their bold abstract designs.

above: BURDEN BASKET

Velveeta Volante (Apache). 1997. Oracle, Arizona. Willow, leather, silver. Courtesy Southwestern Association for Indian Arts, Inc., Santa Fe, New Mexico.

right: VELVEETA HENRY VOLANTE, APACHE BASKET-MAKER.

opposite: STORAGE BASKET

Western Apache. Early 1900s. Arizona. Willow or sumac shoots (foundation), willow shoots, devil's claw, and dyed yucca root (weft). H: 3¼", D: 22". California Academy of Sciences, San Francisco. Catalog #516-14. Photograph by Dong Lin.
The Apache basketmakers who crafted vase-shaped ollas were probably inspired by the forms of Pueblo potters. This outstanding example of the form offers a variety of decorative patterns woven over a three-rod foundation. Small figures of dogs and men punctuate the strong diamond and zigzag patterns, and each row of diamonds is broken by a checkered band.

of Second Mesa, northeast of Flagstaff, who produce coiled baskets as fine as any ever made by their ancestors, and by wicker basketmakers at Third Mesa, who specialize in brightly colored plaques. The Hopi's determined adherence to their traditional way of life has helped shield their basket-making from the too often degenerative influence of the marketplace. Unlike most other contemporary Indian artisans, the Hopi still make baskets for themselves as well as for sale to tourists, and this steadfast refusal to separate the strands of their culture keeps their work rooted, vital, and fresh. Their basketmaking is still an integral part of their culture and identity, not a nostalgic or purely commercial activity intended to recall and capitalize on the glory days of their ancestors.

Although the Hopi are better known among the general public, the finest post-contact basketmakers in the Southwest were the Western Apache. They were latecomers to the region who originated in Canada and arrived in the Southwest only about five hundred years ago. Less war-like and nomadic than other Apache branches, the western tribes, who settled in east central Arizona, practiced agriculture and largely avoided the devastating clashes with whites suffered by their more stubborn and aggressive kin.

Unlike the Hopi and other pueblo-dwelling peoples, the Apache made almost no pottery and were therefore dependent on basketry for carriers and containers. They carefully observed and appropriated the time-honored ways of their neighbors in the region and probably learned basketmaking from the Pueblos. Apache artisans generally coiled and sewed their baskets of peeled shoots of willow or cottonwood and decorated them with black devil's-claw. In addition to their decorative applications, the rugged fibers of devil's-claw could be used to reinforce bases and rims and to make the baskets less porous.

The dominant Western Apache basket forms were shallow bowls made for household use and large ollas, or storage jars. Apache craftspeople probably modeled their ollas after the similarly shaped ceramic water jars made by Pueblo potters throughout the nineteenth and twentieth centuries. The earliest surviving coiled Apache basketry ollas date from the 1880s; most were made around the turn of the century for sale to white collectors. Many Apache ollas are 24 or more inches tall; the largest are approximately 4 feet high. The tall ollas demanded great technical skill and a tremendous investment of time, often taking a year or more to complete. Artisans also wove extremely large bowls, up to 30 inches in diameter, in response to the demand from collectors after the turn of the century. Both types of Apache baskets were decorated with geometric motifs; baskets made for sale were often decorated with many small human and animal figures, which proved popular with early collectors.

Basketmaking traditions in the Southwest, as in other regions across the country, are threatened today not only by outside cultural forces but also by pressures on the environment. The natural materials that made the art possible are increasingly hard to find, and basketmakers often have to travel many miles to gather plants that were widely available locally only a generation ago. Because some people regard them as weeds, these wild plants are also subject to contamination by herbicides and other chemicals. Native basketmaking plants such as devil's-claw, sumac, and even yucca continue to be eradicated by ranchers and farmers, making the craft of basketmaking even more difficult, time-consuming, and expensive.

Despite these and other obstacles, however, hundreds of southwest Indians continue to make traditional baskets, and the art seems alive and reasonably well in the region. Tourist and collector interest in southwestern basketry continues to grow, and the demand for the work of many modern basketmakers is far greater than the supply.

above: BASKET PLAQUE

Hopi. Early twentieth century. Third Mesa, northeastern Arizona. Dyed rabbitbrush and sumac, yucca. Haffenreffer Museum of Anthropology, Brown University, Bristol, Rhode Island.
This brightly colored plaque employs commercial aniline dyes, which were in favor among Hopi weavers in the early years of the twentieth century.

opposite: BURDEN BASKET

Western Apache. Early twentieth century. Arizona. Willow or sumac, leather, tin. H: 38 cm, D: 42 cm. Haffenreffer Museum of Anthropology, Brown University, Bristol, Rhode Island.
Apache women carried baskets like this on their backs as they foraged for wild edibles. Burden baskets were often decorated with strips of rawhide; bits of tin could then be attached to the ends of the rawhide fringe and would tinkle and flash in the sun as the women moved about.

The Southeast

The Southeast—encompassing what is now Tennessee, Louisiana, Mississippi, Alabama, Georgia, Florida, and the Carolinas—was home to some of the most ancient, complex, and advanced Indian civilizations in the Americas. Before contact

above: NESTED SET OF BASKETS

Chitimacha. Late nineteenth century. Avery Island, Louisiana. Natural and dyed river cane. Largest basket: H: 5", L: 4⅝", W: 3¼". Smallest basket: H: 2⅝", L: 2½", W: 1¾". Lauren Rogers Museum of Art, Laurel, Mississippi. Gift of Catherine Marshall Gardiner.

Each basket in this set carries a different twilled decorative pattern. The traditional Chitimacha names for the patterns on the three largest baskets translate as worm track (right center), alligator gut, and muskadine rind (far right). The pattern at far left is called cow eye.

with whites, Native Americans in the Southeast lived in large permanent villages that were often surrounded by wooden walls for protection from attack by rivals. Skilled farmers who took advantage of the region's mild weather and abundant rain, they grew tobacco, corn, beans, melons, sunflowers, and squash. Their primary crop, corn, was eaten fresh and also dried for winter use as meal. Deer provided the main source of meat for the southeast Indians, and most of the region's people wore deerskin clothing.

Spanish explorers first encountered the great agricultural societies of the Southeast in the early sixteenth century, and French and English colonists soon added their own pressures. By 1800 Native American societies had suffered such devastating losses from disease, war, and dislocation that entire civilizations, like the Natchez, had disappeared almost without a trace. Although a similarly tragic pattern continued across the continent during the nineteenth century, the Indians of the Southeast felt the inex-

orable clash of cultures earlier and more profoundly than those in other regions. Successive waves of Spanish, French, and English settlers coveted their land, and by the 1840s the U.S. government had forced most of the region's Indians westward to new homes.

Of the many southeast Indians who made baskets, the two most important basketmaking tribes of the region were the Chitimacha and the Cherokee. The Chitimacha, a small southern Louisiana tribe that still occupies ancestral land in the Mississippi Delta, were the finest and most technically advanced basketmakers in the Southeast. They crafted their baskets of narrow splints cut from the stems of river cane (*Arundinaria tecta*), an herbaceous bamboolike shrub that grew in vast, dense stands along streams and rivers throughout the Southeast. In addition to its importance in basketmaking, the once ubiquitous cane supplied many other needs of regional Indians who fashioned its hollow tubes into building material, arrow and knife shafts, torches, and even blowguns. The

above: UTILITY BASKET

Choctaw. c. 1880-1900. Mississippi. Plain and dyed river cane. H: 6", D: 12". Lauren Rogers Museum of Art, Laurel, Mississippi. Gift of Catherine Marshall Gardiner. Catalog #23.29.
Most Choctaw twill work is single woven, but this example is double woven, like the work of Louisiana's Chitimacha. The square-based basket is decorated with bands of cane dyed yellow and brown.

opposite: HANDLED BASKET

Cherokee or Catawba. Early twentieth century. North Carolina. Natural and dyed river cane with hickory bark rim binding, hickory handle. H: 11½", D: 11". Peabody Museum of Archaeology and Ethnology, Harvard University, Cambridge, Massachusetts. Photograph by Hillel Burger.
This example is twill plaited with three colors of plain and dyed river cane arranged to create diamond-shaped patterns. The bark rim binding distinguishes the basket as Cherokee and Catawba work.

following pages: ZIG-ZAG TWILLED BASKET

Joyce Schaum. 1993. Keymar, Maryland. Hand-dyed rattan. 19" x 16". Private collection. Photo by T. R. Wailes.
Schaum's work often shows the influence of traditional Southeastern Indian basketry, especially that of the Cherokee. She originally worked in stained glass, and many of her twilled baskets are richly colored.

Chitimacha appear to have been the first tribe to use cane in basketmaking, and they remain masters in its use to the present day. Elements of Chitimacha cane basketry influenced neighboring tribes, including the Choctaw and Cherokee, but neither group could surpass the Chitimacha's combined technical and decorative skills.

After Chitimacha craftspeople split and scraped the cane to produce even-sized glossy splints, they positioned the pieces as both the warp and the weft; plaited at right angles to one another, the splints formed a closely spaced two-over-two or three-over-three twill. The finest Chitimacha baskets were double woven, with two layers of twilled plaiting that joined only at the finishing rim edge. Many Chitimacha baskets, which are usually square or rectangular, also had deep, form-fitting lids, woven to match the baskets and typically extending one-third to one-half of the way down the sides of the basket.

Chitimacha baskets are also notable for their intricate designs, created through the use of dyed splints. Artisans colored selected splints of cane with natural dyes before weaving. Boiled walnut root produced a rich black dye, and bloodroot or a combination of Texas oak and black gum tree bark created a deep red. The Chitimacha used the dye pieces in combination with natural tan splints to create diagonal bands of color overlaid with geometric patterns of circles, triangles, squares, four-pointed stars, or running or looping chains, with descriptive names such as "eyes of cattle" and "worm track." These patterns decorated only the outside of a double-woven basket; the inside layer was usually woven entirely of undyed cane.

The Chitimacha tradition is alive today largely through the influence of Ada Thomas, who single-handedly reintroduced the complex double-weave style in the 1970s. Thomas, who learned basketmaking from a grandmother and aunt, shared her knowledge by teaching traditional Chitimacha basketry in a local school and by serving as mentor to younger craftspeople. In 1983 the National Endowment for the Arts Folk Arts Program recognized her as a National Heritage Fellow for her efforts in preserving and reviving the tradition, which might well have been lost without her. The biggest threat to traditional Chitimacha basketry today is a lack of cane, which has been destroyed by development of its wetland habitat.

Another important basketmaking tradition arose among the Cherokee, who originally lived throughout southern Appalachia but were displaced by whites early in the nineteenth century. State governments systematically stripped Indians of their rights and opened their lands to settlement. The Cherokee, however, believed they had a legal right to their ancestral land; they sued to win back land that had been taken from them, and in the late 1820s their hard-fought case finally reached the Supreme Court. Although Chief Justice John Marshall presided over a decision that rendered the challenged state laws unconstitutional, President Andrew Jackson refused to enforce it and instead signed a law in 1830 to remove the Indians. During the following decade, thousands of Cherokee were forcibly and shamefully relocated by the U.S. government to reservations in Oklahoma, which was then known as the Indian Territory. Armed escorts marched them to their new "home" along the infamous Trail of Tears. At least 2,000 of the estimated 16,000 Cherokees who were forced westward on the trail are believed to have died en route.

A small number of the Cherokee, who had previously left the tribe and obtained U.S. citizenship, remained in northwestern North Carolina, exempted from removal by their citizenship. Others became fugitives, hiding in inaccessible parts of the Southern Highlands. Eventually the government purchased reservation land at Cherokee, North Carolina, near Asheville, and allowed both groups of eastern Cherokee to settle on the reservation, where they remain to this day.

Cherokee basketmakers originally worked with river cane, from which they crafted twilled, double-woven baskets for their own ceremonial and utilitarian purposes. During the nineteenth

left: RIBBED BASKET WITH HINGED LID

Probably Cherokee. c. 1920. Found in Franklin County, Tennessee. White oak, natural pigments. Collection of Roddy and Sally Moore. Photograph by Ken Burris.

Although this basket's origin is undocumented, similar examples with a centrally hinged lid and colored splint are known to be made by Cherokee.

below: SWING-HANDLED BASKET WITH LACED BAIL

Elenora and John Wilnoty (Cherokee). c. 1983. Cherokee, North Carolina. Plain and dyed white oak splint, hickory handle. 9½" x 5" x 7". Collection of Cynthia Taylor. Photograph by Ken Burris.

Like a number of contemporary Cherokee artisans, the Wilnotys collaborate on their baskets. John is a woodcarver who fashions the basket handles, while Elenora weaves the baskets. This basket's unusual handle is laced back on itself for added strength.

above: MARKET BASKET

Melinda Taylor. c. 1950. Qualla Indian Reservation, Cherokee, North Carolina. Natural and dyed white oak. Maximum height: 9½". Appalachian Museum, Berea College, Berea, Kentucky.

This Cherokee basket was originally purchased through Allanstand Cottage Industries in Asheville, North Carolina. It was made to be used as a carrier for foods and other goods purchased at local markets.

opposite: DOUBLE WALL BASKET

Cherokee. c. 1930. Western North Carolina. Natural and dyed white oak. H: 19½". Collection of Roddy and Sally Moore. Photograph by Ken Burris.

Like their Northeastern contemporaries, the Cherokee sometimes made tiered wall baskets for sale to tourists. This example includes dyed splint and a diagonal overlay of curlicues, both common in Cherokee trade baskets.

century, however, when they began selling baskets to their white neighbors in Appalachia, the Cherokee switched their primary basket material to oak splint, long the favored material of non-Indian basketmakers in the region. From it they fashioned a variety of forms, including the ribbed baskets crafted by white basketmakers in the Southern Highlands. This sharing of forms, materials, and techniques, brought about by the long regional history of close interaction between the races—including a considerable amount of intermarriage—can at times make it hard to distinguish between white and Cherokee work. Some approaches were unique to the Cherokee, however. Whether working with oak or cane, Cherokee basketmakers often used dyed splints, which are rarely found in early utilitarian baskets made by whites. Many Cherokee baskets in both materials are twill plaited. While twilled baskets of whites or other tribes are often decorated with diamond patterns, the Cherokee commonly used simple alternating rows of colored (usually dark brown or red) and uncolored weavers on their baskets. Some contemporary makers have remastered the art of double-weave twill, creating baskets within baskets similar to those made by the Chitimacha. Unlike those of the Chitimacha, however, most Cherokee baskets have handles rather than lids.

As inexpensive manufactured containers reached the highlands, the Cherokee's white neighbors needed far fewer utilitarian baskets. Resourceful Cherokee women began making purely decorative baskets for sale to the many tourists who came to the region. Tourists liked the colorful, decorative effects possible with honeysuckle and maple, and innovative Cherokee craftswomen developed new forms and techniques that exploited the possibilities of these new materials.

Today, basketmaking is the most important craft practiced by the eastern Cherokee. The Indian-managed Qualla Arts and Crafts Mutual, Inc., cooperative in Cherokee, North Carolina, represents over one hundred Cherokee artisans. The Qualla cooperative is affiliated with the Southern Highland Handicraft Guild in Asheville, which was founded in 1930 as an umbrella organization that unites a large number of Appalachian craft schools and centers and increases recognition of highland crafts. During the 1930s the guild organized seminal craft exhibitions that traveled to major museums around the country and brought contemporary highland work to the attention of many Americans for the first time. It continues to help coordinate the production and marketing of crafts from the region and maintains high standards for traditional highland workmanship, including that of the Cherokee.

Contemporary Cherokee basketmakers are experimenting with a variety of materials and forms, creating distinctive modern twists on traditional themes. Most of today's artisans specialize in one of the four materials used by Cherokee women over the centuries: river cane, white oak, honeysuckle, or red maple. Lengths of the prolific honeysuckle vine, are boiled, stripped of their bark, and then dyed with black walnut husks to produce a deep brownish purple that contrasts boldly with the white color of the peeled, undyed vine. Basketmakers weave honeysuckle in wicker style in a variety of nontraditional forms such as round lidded sewing baskets, wastebaskets, vases, lidded or open-mouthed and jars. Most honeysuckle baskets feature horizontal or vertical bands of dyed weft, and many of the fanciest baskets add a central row of circular twists of dyed weft fiber. Red maple (*Acer rubrum*) is a soft, light wood far better suited to decorative work than oak. The tree has long been among the most common in Appalachia, and, unlike oak, it remains abundant because it is too soft for use for building, furnituremaking, and other commercial purposes. Like northern black ash, red maple can be easily twisted into decorative curls or crosses; it also resembles northern black ash in the satiny sheen of its inside surface, which, when dyed with the often brilliant colors favored by contemporary artisans and their clientele, seems almost to glow.

Cherokee basketmakers continue to balance tradition and change, adapting their art in response to diminishing resources and fickle markets. Despite the difficult economic pressures under which they work, however, the finest Cherokee basketmakers have managed to remain true to their art, and to produce baskets that add to and extend the rich history of this important tribal craft.

The Northeast

The Algonquin Indian tribes of New
England, northern New York, and southern
Canada were the first Native Americans to
be encountered by English and French
explorers and settlers. Their territory, a forest of mixed hardwoods and evergreens,

Greetings from Bar Harbor.

THE INDIAN VILLAGE.

above: C. 1885 POSTCARD OF THE INDIAN VILLAGE AT BAR HARBOR, Abbe Museum, Bar Harbor, Maine. Indian basketmakers gathered at Bar Harbor and other New England resorts during the summer months to sell their wares to tourists.

stretched unbroken from the Atlantic coast of New England to the Great Lakes and the Mississippi River, and extended as far south as northern Virginia and Tennessee.

Early New England Indians lived a seminomadic life closely linked to the annual cycle of the region's weather. They moved to different sites during the year to hunt, fish, gather berries, or grow crops, taking advantage of seasonal events such as spawning runs, migratory flights, and even snow cover, which made it easier to track animals. Although Indians in northern New England generally did not practice agriculture, those in Massachusetts, Connecticut, Rhode Island, and southern Maine, New Hampshire, and Vermont took significant advantage of the area's longer frost-free growing season. During the warmer months, the southern Indians, who constituted 80 percent of New England's native population, gathered together to grow such indigenous American crops as corn, pumpkins, squash, beans, and tobacco. During the long, cold winters they

left: FANCY BASKET
Probably Passamaquoddy. c. 1950–70. Eastport, Maine area. Plain and dyed ash splint, sweetgrass. H: 15 cm., D: 18 cm. Terry Collection, Unity College, Unity, Maine.
Some of the ash spint used to make this porcupine weave fancy basket was dipped into green dye to achieve a light wash of color.

broke up into smaller groups and hunted for deer, moose, and bear.

Interaction between whites and Indians has been an important part of the region's history since the early 1600s when the whites first settled in the Northeast. By the mid-1800s, however, disease and restricted movement necessitated by the whites' permanent settlements and land ownership severely reduced the Native American population. Indians now lived primarily on reservations, areas of largely undesirable land set aside by whites. Deprived of their former freedom to move about and thereby support themselves, they depended increasingly on trade with their white neighbors to supply their needs.

Throughout the nineteenth and early twentieth centuries, New England Indians such as the Micmac, Schagticoke, Penobscot, Mohegan, Passamaquoddy, Pequot, and Wampanoag made baskets for their own use. Basketmaking also became one of the main crafts that New England Indians practiced to sell to or barter with whites. Early in the nineteenth

preceding pages, left:

TOURIST BASKET

Abenaki. Early twentieth century. Probably northern Vermont. Dyed willow and sweet grass. H: 12⅜", D: 10¼". Hood Museum of Art, Dartmouth College, Hanover, New Hampshire. Gift of Glover Street Hastings III.

Barrel-shaped forms like this were woven over a wooden mold and were made by a number of northern New England tribes. The form was popular with tourists, but was never used by Native Americans.

preceding pages, right:

SWING-HANDLED BASKET

Unknown New England Indian. c. 1960. New England. Natural and dyed black ash. H: 14", D: 17". Shelburne Museum, Shelburne, Vermont. Photograph by Ken Burris.

A bold decorative band of curled dyed splint and a looped swing handle distinguish this modern basket.

century, Indian basketmakers peddled their wares from door to door, offering storage and work baskets that were popular with white farmers, storekeepers, and homeowners. Beginning in the 1870s, Indians living near popular new spa and resort areas such as Bar Harbor and Poland Spring, Maine, and the White Mountains of New Hampshire began to make smaller fancy baskets to sell to tourists. Fancy baskets catered to Victorian taste by combining a wide range of largely European forms with such special Native American decorative touches as braided sweetgrass embellishments, protruding porcupine weaves, and intricately shaped handles.

Whether functional or fancy, the vast majority of New England Indian baskets were woven from thin, flat strips of wood called splint, which the basketmakers wove over and under each other at right angles. The origins of splint basketry in the New World remain unclear, but historians know that splint baskets were common in Europe, and immigrants brought knowledge of splint craftsmanship with them. However, the survival of a few very early splint basket fragments may be proof that Indians understood the principles of splint basketry before contact with Europeans. The origins of certain basketmaking techniques also remain unclear, since Indians and whites constantly learned from and influenced each other. Early Shaker communities, for example, obtained baskets and basketmaking materials from the Indians; they later modified and improved on the traditional Indian forms.

Whatever its origin and early history, by 1800 splint baskets were the only type made by New England Indians, many of whom prepared their "basket stuff" from black ash, a common northeastern tree that provides a strong but pliable weaving material. They also sometimes prepared splint from other local hardwoods, including oak, hickory, and maple. Basketmakers worked with splint while it was still green, allowing it to dry out only after a basket was complete. Prior to the mid-1800s, craftspeople cut and prepared the lengths of ash splint with straight and draw knives, which often resulted in splint weavers of uneven widths. Indians also tended to use lighter-weight splint than whites, and as a result, their baskets were often less substantial and less sturdy.

The earliest New England Indian splint baskets were square or rectangular, and because many were used for storage, lids were a common feature. Artisans decorated early baskets with brightly colored abstract or geometric

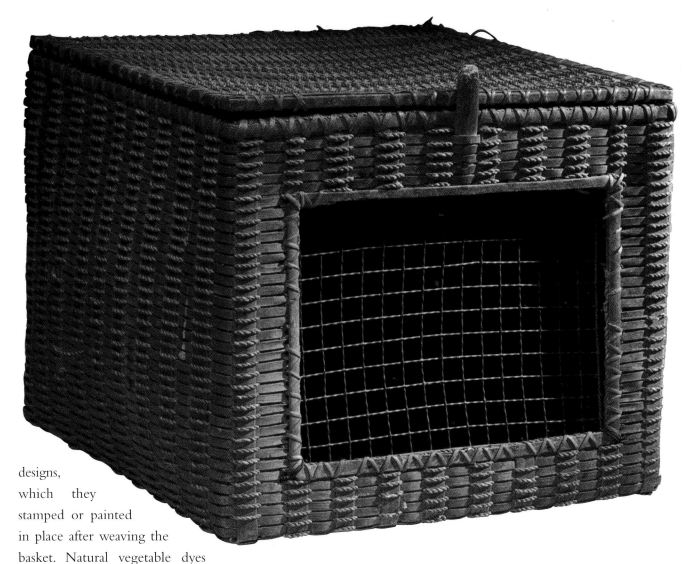

designs,
which they
stamped or painted
in place after weaving the
basket. Natural vegetable dyes
such as indigo (*Indigofera* sp.), walnut hulls, or the red berries of Solomon's
seal (*Polyganatum* sp.), or commercial dry pigments mixed with water and
animal-hide glue were often used to color the splint. A mixture of red and
white lead, which produced what is now called Mohegan pink, was particularly popular, partly because the materials were inexpensive. Indians typically applied the dye only to the outside face of the splint, so that the
interior and bottom of the basket remained plain. They often wove dyed
and undyed splint together to create horizontal bands or patterns of color;
they also combined colored splint with stamped or painted designs to produce vividly decorated surfaces.

above: POULTRY CAGE
*John T. Ronco. c. 1910. Old Town, Maine. Black
ash, sweetgrass, wire. H: 16", W: 15½". Shelburne
Museum, Shelburne, Vermont. Photograph by Ken
Burris.*
This unusual basket cage may have been
used to transport chickens or ducks to
market. The basket's lid is secured with a
wooden peg at the front.

Collecting

NORTHEASTERN Indian baskets can be divided into two broad categories: utilitarian baskets made for use by Indians or sale to their white neighbors, and the later decorative fancy baskets made strictly for sale to tourists. Relatively few early baskets have survived; any made before 1850 are rare and highly coveted by collectors. Because they were made in greater quantities and suffered far less from daily wear and tear, fancy baskets are far more common than earlier utilitarian examples, thus the quality of their workmanship rather than their rarity governs the prices. Good examples in both categories cost several hundred dollars, while the rarest and choicest early examples, such as large, lidded storage baskets with extensive, well-preserved decoration can easily bring more than ten times as much.

Painted decoration is the hallmark of early northeastern baskets. Rich hues cover some, while others are decorated with dyed weavers, stamps, or stencils. Vibrant reds, pinks, yellows, greens, and blues are common, and contrast beautifully with areas or patterns of uncolored ash splint. Many different northeastern tribes created baskets with distinctive decorative techniques and motifs, which can

be the subject of much study and enjoyment. Some connoisseurs focus on the products of a particular tribal group such as the Schagticoke or Penobscot; others collect by region, searching for examples from a specific state, or from a production center such as Old Town, Maine, or Brothertown, New York. Collectors also cherish work by certain craftspeople, such as the well-known late nineteenth-century Schagticoke artisan Henry "Hen Pen" Harris.

Northeastern Indian baskets reflect the interaction of Native Americans and European settlers better than those of any other region. As commerce increased between the two groups in the nineteenth century, Indians adapted their baskets to suit the tastes of their customers, so as a rule, the older the basket, the purer its Indian sensibility. The best fancy baskets strike a balance between traditional Indian techniques and color combinations and the wonderful decorative excess of Victorian design.

above: BASKET
Mohegan. Early nineteenth century. Brothertown, New York. Natural and dyed black ash. H: 4", L: 7½", W: 4½". Haffenreffer Museum of Anthropology, Brown University, Bristol, Rhode Island.

Brothertown was a settlement on Indian-owned lands near Oneida in upstate New York. Certain New England Mohegans voluntarily emigrated to Brothertown in the late eighteenth and early nineteenth centuries, where they absorbed decorative techniques of other tribes living there. This early basket is typical of Mohegan work in its exclusive use of wide splint and its brightly colored medallion designs.

Basketmakers usually wove fancy baskets over carved wooden molds, which allowed them to achieve a tighter weave and to replicate the same basket form again and again. Artisans could craft small or odd shapes much more easily over a mold as well. Most makers of fancy baskets cut their splint with a gauge, a simple tool made by setting a row of metal teeth into a short handle. Using a gauge, a basketmaker could cut a strip of prepared splint into several narrow lengths of precisely the same width. Molds and gauges greatly facilitated commercial production work and helped ensure uniform quality from basket to basket.

Makers of fancy baskets created a wide range of forms for their customers, including small acorn-shaped yarn baskets, pack baskets, handbags,

above: THE CHIEF MAURICE DENNIS FAMILY OF BASKET-MAKERS, photographed near Old Forge, New York, c. 1920. Indian basket-makers often donned costumes to help sales to their tourist customers.
Adirondack Museum, Blue Mountain Lake, New York.

shopping bags, multitiered hanging wall pockets, compartmentalized sewing baskets, covered trinket baskets, wastebaskets, hampers, tiny strawberry-shaped baskets, bread baskets, and trays. In order to catch the tourist's eye and create a pleasing visual effect, the craftspeople added elaborate designs to many of their baskets. In some fancy baskets, artisans juxtaposed splint of different widths and colors to create distinctive horizontal patterns. Coastal Maine Indians sometimes incorporated dyed braided sweetgrass into the weave as an embellishment. But undoubtedly the aptly named porcupine work was the most popular and distinctive embellishment used by the northeastern basketmakers. Created by looping or twisting the splint before passing it over a vertical element that projected out from the surface, the "quills" could also be flattened or pointed to suit the artisan's vision or the customer's whim. A fancy basket covered with rows of decorative quills or curlicues, as many were, resembled the bristly, prickly look of an alarmed porcupine. Porcupine work was especially popular on small decorative ladies' baskets made in the last decades of the nineteenth century.

In the late nineteenth and early twentieth centuries, Indians in many areas of the Northeast formed basketmaking cooperatives. In addition to making baskets for direct sale to the tourist market, some of the cooperatives sold to white middlemen, who in turn marketed the baskets through regional department stores and mail-order catalogs. Some of the cooperatives were so well known that they became tourist destinations in their own right.

Demand for northeastern Indian baskets fell drastically during the Depression. Fewer people could afford to take vacations and buy souvenirs, and tastes also changed dramatically, moving away from the fussy old-fashioned quaintness of the late Victorian era and toward the spare industrial designs and man-made materials of the Art Deco era. Traditional handcrafts fell out of fashion. After World War II, the introduction of inexpensive plastic containers combined with a flood of cheap imported baskets to doom the northeastern Indian basketmaking industry. For the few Indians who still create traditional splint baskets today, the craft is an avocation rather than a means of livelihood. Fancy baskets continue to dominate production, but some northeastern artisans also make utilitarian forms such as hampers, laundry baskets, and potato baskets.

opposite: EARED BASKET
Northeastern Indian. Early twentieth century. New England or New York. Natural and dyed ash, applied stamps. H: 6¼", D: 10". Shelburne Museum, Shelburne, Vermont. Photograph by Ken Burris.
This little household basket is decorated with alternating bands of dyed splint and embellished with repeated stamps that form a pattern of broken crosses.

Part II

Immigrant Traditions

New England

above: CHILD'S BASKET
Artist unknown. c. 1880. Probably Connecticut. Stained white oak splint with hardwood handle. Overall height: 6¾", W: 6", L: 6¾". Private collection.
This well-proportioned little basket has a thin, delicate handle made to fit a child's hand. Southern New England basketmakers occasionally used white oak rather than ash as their "basket stuff."

left: BLACK ASH BASKETMAKER JONATHAN KLINE preparing splint from a basket log.

opposite: PACK BASKET
Jonathan Kline. 1995. Trumansburg, New York. Black ash and hickory. H. (including handle) 21", dimensions of opening 16" x 13". Private collection.
Often called Adirondack pack baskets, baskets like this were common throughout the north woods and favored by trappers and canoeists. The baskets, which were made by both white and Indian artisans, were typically fitted with adjustable leather or canvas carrying straps. Heavy splint was used to withstand the wear and tear of hard use. Kline comments, "Many traditional shapes exist. I particularly like this bellied form."

preceding pages, right: NANTUCKET BASKETMAKER CLINTON MITCHELL "MITCHY" RAY shaving staves with a draw knife in his shop, c. 1950. (Detail.)
Nantucket Historical Association, Nantucket, Massachusetts.

New England comprises six states of widely varied terrain, ranging from the rolling farmlands of inland Maine, Massachusetts, Connecticut, and Rhode Island to the sandy dunes of Cape Cod to the White and Green Mountains to the rock-

above: CHEESE BASKET
*Artist unknown. c. 1900. Vermont. Ash. H: 8",
D: 20½". Shelburne Museum, Shelburne,
Vermont. Photograph by Ken Burris.*
Basketmakers created the hexagonal
openwork weave of cheese baskets by
weaving opposing diagonals over and
under horizontal strips of the same size
splint.

bound Down East coast. As its name indicates, immigrants from England,
dominated by Puritan Protestants from East Anglia, settled the area. The
hardworking, intensely religious, and morally upright Puritans formed
tight communities that valued forbearance and interdependence. They
found the rocky soil and long, hard winters of the region both challenging
and rewarding, and their tough, resourceful character become inseparably
intertwined with the land on which they grew and flourished. Once the

above: WINNOWING BASKET
Artist unknown. c. 1870. Vermont. Willow, wood-splint lashings, leather lining. W: 33", D: 37". Shelburne Museum, Shelburne, Vermont. Photograph by Ken Burris.
Lightweight willow was often used to craft bulky winnowing baskets.

settlers had removed boulders and leveled forests, the gently rolling countryside of New England offered ideal farmland.

On the typical New England homestead, handmade baskets served dozens of different purposes, providing containers for gathering, processing, measuring, and storing food and other materials. Unlike wooden containers, baskets had the great advantage of being lightweight.

New England baskets took many utilitarian forms. Sturdy double-handled workbaskets were essential for harvesting apples, potatoes, and other fruits and vegetables as well as for storing them in the root cellar during the long winter. Famers used enormous shallow oval baskets to winnow grain; they often lined these baskets with leather to prevent the grains of wheat or rye from escaping. After cutting and threshing the grain to separate the husks and stalks from the kernels, they scooped the grain into the winnowing basket and tossed it into the air near a breezy barn doorway; the heavier grain fell back into the basket while lighter chaff was blown away.

right: WIRE-HANDLED BASKET
Cemore Landon Morehouse. c. 1880. Westford,
Vermont. Ash with wire and hardwood handle.
D: 6¾". Shelburne Museum, Shelburne, Vermont.
Photograph by Ken Burris.
Morehouse (1822–1909) was Vermont's
most accomplished and versatile
nineteenth-century basketmaker. This
unusual little basket combines the wire
bail handle of a tin pail with a traditional
basket form.

preceding pages: EEL TRAP
Artist unknown. c. 1880. Ash, hardwood, rope.
L: 25". New England. Shelburne Museum,
Shelburne, Vermont. Photograph by Ken Burris.
This simply made but effective trap was
probably crafted by a Native American.
Similar traps were used by both Indians
and whites in the Northeast.

Baskets were also essential in animal husbandry. Most landowners and small farmers in the region kept a dairy cow for their own use and made cheese by fermenting the milk. When the milk formed curds of cheese, the farmers strained them from the remaining liquid whey by pouring the mixture into a porous open-weave basket lined with cheesecloth. Farmers used small, round baskets with raised bases to cradle freshly laid eggs, and they had other types of baskets for transporting chickens, geese, turkeys, and pigeons safely to market. Farmers often placed a vase-shaped basket over a goose's head while they plucked its insulating down feathers, a task that invariably provoked the fowl's temper and put the plucker at some risk. Covered feather baskets served to keep plucked down and feathers from blowing away. Feather baskets often had lids that slid up and down on the upright handle, enabling the gatherer to raise the lid and tuck feathers

above: DOUBLE SWING-HANDLED
MARKET BASKET
*Jonathan Kline. 1995. Trumansburg, New York.
Black ash splint, shagbark hickory handles and runners. H: 9½", W: 13", L: 19". Private collection.*
Hardwood runners secured along the
length of the bottom protect its plaited
rectangular weave. The sides are woven
straight, while the top keeps the rectangular form.

inside easily with one hand. Baskets also held wool before and after the farm wife carded and spun it. Inside the house, baskets were used to hold thread, scraps of cloth, other sewing supplies, and small personal items, and to carry laundry between the washtub and the clothesline.

New Englanders also used baskets to carry fish, clams, oysters, mussels, and crabs home or to market. Lidded creels shaded fish from the drying sun at the same time they allowed air to flow freely; they kept trout, salmon, and panfish cool and fresh until the fisherman reached his destination. And freshwater eels, a popular staple in early days, were trapped in long, cylindrical baskets with a narrow, funnel-shaped opening at one end and a wooden plug at the other. The fishermen would put some dead fish

in the trap to serve as bait and point the narrow entrance downstream. Eels, smelling the bait, would squeeze through the tight opening of the trap and would not be able to escape back through the funnel.

Since baskets were used as measuring devices for foods, herbs, wool, and other materials, New England basketmakers made them in sizes ranging from a bushel down to a pint. Most measuring baskets are square or rectangular and employ splint construction, in which thin horizontal weavers are laced through a framework of wider vertical stakes. Northeastern makers occasionally created round or oval splint baskets, which demanded more technical skill and are therefore less common. Most splint baskets were constructed with a plain weave—over-one, under-one, set in alternating rows. The craftsmen reinforced the bases of square and rectangular baskets with interwoven stakes and strengthened the foundations of round and oval splint baskets with interwoven weavers and stakes. In both cases, they turned up the splints to form the side framework after finishing the bottom. Once the sides were woven, they lashed a thick bentwood rim in place. A handle or handles, which an artisan could add last or incorporate into the framework as stakes, finished the basket. The most common types included curved overhead handles, followed by "eared" handles—grips set into opposite sides of the basket. The least common and most difficult to execute were swing handles, which were attached to side pivots so that they could be moved up and down.

New England settlers were strongly influenced by the Indian traditions that surrounded them; they learned directly from their Indian neighbors or borrowed their techniques and forms. Because interaction, cooperation, and intermarriage between the two groups were common in the region from the earliest days of contact, northeastern Indian and Anglo-American baskets are sometimes difficult to tell apart. To further complicate identification, during the nineteenth and early twentieth centuries, Indians also made undecorated, functional baskets for sale or barter to farmers

opposite: NEW ENGLAND FARM BASKETS

Artists unknown. c. 1860–1880. New England. black ash, hardwood handles. Shelburne Museum, Shelburne, Vermont. Photograph by Ken Burris. A selection of typical nineteenth-century New England farm baskets on exhibit in the kitchen of the historic Dutton House at the Shelburne Museum, Shelburne, Vermont.

below: UTILITY BASKET

Artist unknown. c. 1840. New England. Painted black ash splint with carved hardwood handles. H: 7", W: 5", L: 9¼". Private collection. Photograph courtesy David A. Schorsch American Antiques. This beautifully proportioned little basket was probably used to hold sewing materials and other household sundries.

right: CHEESE BASKET WITH
CARVED BAIL HANDLE

*Artist. unknown c. 1830. New England. Painted
wood splint with carved hardwood handle. H: 11",
W: 10", L: 9½". Private collection. Photograph
courtesy David A. Schorsch American Antiques.*
An atypical hexagonal-weave cheese basket, unusual for its tall, narrow form, bail
handle, and painted surface.

throughout the region, and they also prepared and sold basketmaking
materials that white artisans used.

The dominant basketmaking tree of the Northeast has always been the
black ash (*Fraximus nigra*), also known as hoop or basket ash because of its
common use in fashioning barrel hoops and baskets. The various species of
ash trees, especially the black ash and white ash (*Fraximus americana*), have
long been of considerable economic importance to the region. In addition
to its use in basketmaking, the hard, clean-burning wood makes ideal firewood; deer browse the twigs for food in late winter; and bees visit the
flowers for their pollen. Indians tapped ashes for their sap, which they
boiled down into a dark, bitter sugar. And ash trees, particularly the white
ash, provide a high-quality, straight-grained, and durable lumber that was
used for snowshoes and canoe paddles and is still widely used for furniture,
tool handles, baseball bats, skis, and a host of other purposes.

The moisture-loving black ash is a lowland tree that grows throughout the northeastern United States and southern Canada in swamps and bottomlands, the rich alluvial soil areas found near and along rivers, lakes, and streams. The tree is often called brown ash in northern New England, particularly in Maine, where some basketmakers contradict botanists and claim it is a different species entirely from the black ash of other states. Aforementioned Maine basketmaker Stephen Zeh says that unlike black ash, brown ash likes its feet wet. "Botanically, they may be the same species," he explains, "but there's definitely a difference—inside. Brown ash has so much water that even way down in the heartwood it will squirt out when you pound it. It's like the watermelon of wood."[11] Certainly, the select young trees favored for basketmaking are different from the ordinary black ash, but in any case, the tree provides a superb basketmaking material, at once strong and pliant, which Indian and white craftspeople alike in the region have used for many generations.

Northeastern basketmakers scoured swamps and bottomlands in late winter for rare stands of black ash, using their experience and intuition to decide which trees would provide the best material for their craft. To qual-

below: BUCKBOARD BASKET
Artist unknown. c. 1880. Ash, milk paint. 8" x 26" x 36". Shelburne Museum, Shelburne, Vermont. Photograph by Ken Burris.
Long, shallow, rectangular baskets with open-weave bottoms were used to carry loads in a horse-drawn buckboard wagon or as trays in which to dry fruit and vegetables.

ify as a good basketmaking prospect, a tree had to be young; have a straight trunk free of scars, knots, and other blemishes; and measure roughly a handsbreadth in diameter. Once discovered, after a search that could take days, the location of a fine stand of trees was the basketmaker's most closely guarded secret. Many artisans considered the search for good basket trees the most difficult and critical part of the basketmaking process. For some it was a quasi-religious ritual.

A basketmaker cut a suitable tree into short sections, stripping sections of their bark, and pounding them with a mallet or the butt of an ax until the growth rings separated from each other to form long strips that ran along the grain of the wood. This tendency to separate is unique to ash and sometimes occurs naturally in fallen trees. Native Americans undoubtedly noticed this phenomenon, and it may have first inspired them to use ash as a basketmaking material. After the craftspeople separated the growth rings, they trimmed and split the strips into thin ribbons that were quite flexible and not easily broken. Once a basketmaker started a split, he or she could pull the strands apart by holding one side in each hand and applying slow and steady outward pressure or by pulling apart the splint against the sides of a wooden vise held between the legs. The inner faces of the resulting ribbons of ash were smooth and silky and required no further finishing, but the craftsperson had to scrape smooth the rough and grainy outside edge with a knife. Generally, the satiny inside face of the splint formed the outside of the basket.

Basketmaking was widely practiced in New England throughout the nineteenth and early twentieth centuries, but it had essentially ended by the close of World War II. During the 1930s and 1940s the decline of small family farms in the region combined with the increased availability of metal and plastic containers to render traditional baskets all but obsolete. The past twenty-five years, however, have seen a strong and sustained revival of traditional basketmaking in the Northeast. Dozens of skilled artisans have taken up the trade, and basketmaking demonstrations and workshops are being offered by many museums, community colleges, and school programs. A key figure in the revival, and the grand old man of traditional New England basketmaking, is Newton Washburn of Littleton, New Hampshire. He learned his trade from his mother, who specialized in Indian-influenced fancy baskets. Washburn's great-grandfather, Gilman

above: MAINE BASKETMAKER STEPHEN ZEH

opposite: GROUP OF MAINE ASH SPLINT BASKETS
Stephen Zeh. 1997. Temple, Maine. Maine "brown" ash. Diameter of rear basket: 18"; front basket: 1¼". Private collection.
A sampling of Stephen Zeh's wide-ranging repertoire, including both traditional forms and forms of his own design. From the rear: bushel corn basket, feather-gathering basket with sliding lid, lidded swing-handled basket, "tea" basket, eared and swing-handled potato baskets, French bread basket, mini swing-handled basket.

preceding pages: HOODED CRADLE
Joyce Schaum. 1996. Keymar, Maryland. Plain-woven rattan, cherry base and rockers. 24" x 21" x 35". Private collection. Photograph by T. R. Wailes.
Native American, Appalachian, and New England artisans occasionally crafted basket cradles, although few added rockers to the woven cradle. This refined modern example of the form is woven from rattan rather than ash or oak and sits on an elegant cherry base with rockers.

opposite: FIELD BASKET
Artist unknown. c. 1860. New England. Painted black ash splint with carved hardwood handles. Overall height: 16"; diameter 20". Photograph courtesy David A. Schorsch American Antiques.
New England farmers used deep round baskets like this to harvest corn, potatoes, and other heavy crops. Paint was not only decorative but also protected hard-used outdoor baskets from rot. The unusually long tails of the handles extend to the base of the basket.

Sweetser, was the son of a Swiss immigrant father and an Abenaki mother, and the Sweetser family's basketmaking, which can be traced back to the mid-1800s, has always combined Native American and immigrant approaches.[12] Washburn has been particularly important as a teacher, inspiring and instructing many younger enthusiasts over the years and providing a living link with the region's basketmaking traditions.

Jonathan Kline of Trumansburg, New York, is perhaps the most outstanding of Newt Washburn's nearly sixty apprentices. Kline is a full-time basketmaker who crafts a wide range of traditional utilitarian forms, including such unusual large types as pack baskets, laundry baskets, and tall covered clothes hampers. He also fashions miniatures, including nested sets of six to eight tiny swing-handled baskets that fit comfortably in the palm of one's hand. In recent years Kline has painted many of his baskets, adding an appealing surface to his classic traditional forms. He soaks the baskets in a bark tannin solution to stain the light-colored ash an uneven brown; then he paints them with thin, solid-colored washes of muted blue, green, or red mineral pigment. The resulting surfaces are subtle and often variegated, with areas of stain showing through the sometimes translucent washes of paint to pleasing effect.

Another outstanding contemporary northeastern artisan is the aforementioned Stephen Zeh of Temple, Maine. Zeh, a former trapper who learned his craft from a Penobscot Indian basketmaker named Eddie Newell, has been crafting baskets full-time since the mid-1970s. Zeh, a fastidious Yankee craftsman, often quotes his mentor's admonition that there is "only one way to make a basket, and that is the hard way." He makes traditional round and rectangular baskets in many different sizes, specializing in round swing-handled baskets with carved, pegged handles attached at right angles to ears set on either side of the rim. Like Jonathan Kline, Zeh makes pack baskets as well as nesting sets of three, five, or seven swing-handled baskets.

The Shakers

above: APPLE BASKET
Unknown Shaker artist. 1858. New Lebanon, New York. Ash, hardwood handle, maple cleats on bottom, copper rivets. H: 15", D: 13". Hancock Shaker Village, Hancock, Massachusetts. Photograph by Paul Rocheleau.
A closeup of the basket at left on page 123. This backlit photo emphasizes the basket's fine, even weave as well as its remarkable, virtually unused condition. "Ministry 1858" is written on its bottom, indicating it was used in the Mount Lebanon community's ministry building.

left: SHAKER BASKETMAKER GERRIE KENNEDY demonstrating in the Ministry Shop at Hancock Shaker Village, Hancock, Massachusetts.
Photograph by M. Fredericks courtesy Hancock Shaker Village.

opposite: LIDDED SEWING ACCESSORY BASKETS
Attributed to Elder Daniel Boler. c. 1870. New Lebanon, New York. Black ash. Larger basket: H: 4½", D: 4". The Kentucky Museum, Western Kentucky University, Bowling Green, Kentucky.
Daniel Boler was an elder in the Central Ministry at Mount Lebanon from 1852–1892, where he also oversaw the basketmaking shop for many years. He and his father were originally members of the community at South Union, Kentucky, which they left in 1814, and Boler revisited his old home at least once, in 1852. These small fancy baskets may have come to South Union as samples or gifts.

The Shakers, the best known and most successful of America's many nineteenth-century utopian societies, created some of the century's finest baskets. Made both for their own use and for sale to outsiders, the Shakers' modest but remarkable baskets

above: SEWING BASKET

Unknown Shaker Sister. c. 1880. New Lebanon, New York. Black ash, silk ribbons, and strawberry. Private collection. Photograph courtesy of Richard and Betty Ann Rasso, East Chatham, New York. Made under the supervision of Elder Daniel Boler, this delicate little kitten-head basket is the only one of its type known with sewing attachments.

combine felicitous use of materials with superb craftsmanship. Shaker baskets were widely admired for their practicality and grace in their own time, and many modern basketmakers consider them a paradigm of integrity and quality that can guide their own efforts.

Not unlike the products of Shaker artisans, the beginnings of the Shaker order were at once humble and ambitious. In 1774 an illiterate English factory worker and visionary named Ann Lee, along with the other eight members of a breakaway Quaker sect called the United Society of Believers in Christ's Second Appearing, set sail for America to practice their newly founded religion without persecution and to seek converts for their small flock. The group eventually settled near Albany, New York, in Niskayuna, later renamed Watervliet, where they began to preach their gospel of celibacy, pacifism, hard work, discipline, and worship. The new religion began to take hold in the 1790s, and by 1800 eleven self-sustaining communities of Believers, as they originally called themselves, existed in New England, from Watervliet east to Sabbathday Lake, Maine, and south to Enfield, Connecticut. At the religion's peak in the 1840s, some 4,000 to 6,000 Believers lived in eighteen communities extending as far south and west as Kentucky and Ohio.

Dubbed Shaking Quakers, or Shakers, for the ecstatic, twitching movements they made during worship services, Believers sought to establish heaven on earth. They lived and worked cooperatively, shared all property in common, and practiced self-sufficiency wherever they deemed it practical, building their own dwellings, barns, and workshops; growing their own food; and crafting their own furniture, clothing, tools, boxes, baskets, and other goods. Celibate Shaker Brothers and Sisters lived in Families, sharing rooms in large communal houses with others of the same sex; Brothers and Sisters entered the buildings through separate doorways, climbed separate staircases, and slept on opposite sides of a divided central hall.

The Shakers saw no separation between faith and action, though. Following Mother Ann's dictum, "Put your hands to work, and your hearts to God," they carried their religious beliefs into their daily relations, chores, and crafts. They saw work as a form of worship and attempted to achieve perfection in everything they did, including craftwork. Extremely efficient, Shakers used time deliberately, without either haste or dalliance, in recognition of Mother Ann's philosophy: "Do all your work as though you had a thousand years to live on earth and as you would if you knew you must die tomorrow."

Shaker crafts, including basketmaking, embody the basic tenets of the Shaker faith. Shaker products were ingenious, carefully made, sturdy, harmonious, and above all, plain. Because Shakers separated themselves from the outside world, they were relatively free from the stylistic influences and time pressures of the industrial revolution and were therefore able to define beauty in their own unique way. Working only to supply their own needs, early Shaker craftsmen focused solely on function. Believing that beauty rests on utility—a principle later adopted by modernist architects and craftsmen—the Shakers saw beauty in those objects that functioned best. Whereas products made in the outside world were often prized for their decorative elements—the carved ball-and-claw foot of a Chippendale chair, for example, or the punched or painted designs of a Pennsylvania German tin coffeepot—the Shakers considered decoration unnecessary. (They did not oppose vivid color, however, and often covered furniture and woodwork with rich, solid-color paint or stain made from natural materials.) By eliminating surface decoration from their design vocabulary, Shaker craftspeople reduced every object to its essence and allowed the form, color, pattern, line, and proportion to speak instead.

Baskets served a variety of important functions within the Shaker communities, nearly all of which practiced basketmaking. Small groups of Shakers worked together in the community's basket shop, crafting baskets to meet their own specific needs. Like their worldly neighbors, the Shakers produced baskets intended for making cheese; gathering fruits, vegetables, and herbs; carrying wood chips and other kindling; toting and sorting laundry; and holding sewing materials and small personal accessories.

However, Shaker basketmakers sought to improve upon the baskets made by other settlers and Native Americans, most of which they found

following pages: APPLE BASKETS
Unknown Shaker artists. c. 1850–1860. Left: probably Canterbury, New Hampshire; Others: probably Mount Lebanon, New York. Black ash, hardwood handle, copper tacks. Hancock Shaker Village, Hancock, Massachusetts. Photograph by Paul Rocheleau.
Square-bottomed work baskets of this type were used in Shaker orchards and undoubtedly found many other uses around the village as well. The baskets' bottoms were often reinforced with hardwood cleats. This photo was taken in one of Hancock Shaker Village's historic buildings.

above: COVERED KNIFE BASKET

Unknown Shaker artist. c. 1880. Probably New Lebanon, New York. Black ash with hardwood handle. Overall H: 9⅞", L: 11½", W: 4⅞". Hancock Shaker Village, Pittsfield, Massachusetts. Photograph by Paul Rocheleau.

This type of fancy basket was intended to store kitchen knives and other tableware, but undoubtedly found many uses around the home. The hinged lids (called covers by the Shakers) of this skillfully crafted example are woven with a decorative twilled pattern. Like all Shaker fancy work, this basket was woven over a wooden mold.

inferior. Like most other basketmakers in the region, northeastern Shakers made their baskets from black ash splint. Building on traditional models and methods, they refined the forms and techniques of earlier Indian and northeastern farm baskets by creating perfectly symmetrical shapes and attending to the fine details of construction. For example, early Shaker basketmakers took extra time to finish their rims and handles with files, which allowed finer shaping and a smoother surface. They lined their chip baskets with leather or cloth to hold dirt and small pieces, thereby keeping their indoor spaces clean, and they attached wooden "skates" to the bases so they could drag or slide heavy loads over frozen ground or ice. The lining and the skates also helped to keep the kindling dry. The bottoms of the

Unknown Shaker Brother. c. 1820–1850. Probably Alfred or Sabbathday Lake, Maine. Black ash with hardwood handles. H: 14½", D: 22". United Society of Shakers, Sabbathday Lake, Maine. Photograph by Paul Rocheleau.
Big sturdy baskets like this were used to harvest crops such as potatoes and apples. The basket's bottom is reinforced with a thick piece of splint for extra carrying strength.

following pages: VICTORIAN LAUNDRY BASKET
Joyce Schaum. 1993. Keymar, Maryland. Rattan with oak handles. 16" x 24" x 24". Private collection. Photograph by David Egan.
This large utilitarian basket combines twill and plain weave techniques, adding sophisticated visual appeal to a functional piece. Schaum is best known for her twill weaving, which is influenced by the fancy work of Shaker Sisters. While this basket does not have a direct Shaker antecedent, its combination of beauty and utility is very much in keeping with the Shaker aesthetic.

Shakers' workbaskets were often reinforced, outside and sometimes inside as well, with hardwood strips, which relieved stress on the most vulnerable part of the basket. Craftsmen often used wooden molds to enable them to replicate a perfected basket or handle, and because they equated moral development with technological progress, the Shakers adopted and even devised new methods and tools that saved time and improved the quality of their work. A Shaker sister is credited, for example, with the invention of the circular saw, in 1810. Later Shaker basketmakers modified blacksmiths' trip-hammers for use in pounding the splint from ash logs. They also used mechanical tools to shape uniform handles and rims.

Shakers freely shared information, ideas, and craft products with other

above: BASKET MOLDS

Unknown Shaker artists. c. 1840–1850. Front: Community unknown. White pine. 4⅛" x 2½". Center: probably Hancock, Massachusetts, or Mount Lebanon, New York. Birch. 3" x 3¾" Rear: probably Mount Lebanon, New York. Hemlock. 4" x 4¼". Hancock Shaker Village, Hancock, Massachusetts. Photograph by Paul Rocheleau.

Molds were particularly useful in maintaining the forms of the Shakers' small decorative fancy baskets, which required tight weaving with extremely fine splint. The molds were usually carved from the soft wood of pine or other conifers.

communities, and the Elders regularly traveled from village to village, observing different communities' solutions to common problems and spreading Shaker innovations. Brothers and Sisters also occasionally moved from one community to another, bringing products and ideas with them from their home villages, and converts inevitably brought fresh skills and influences to the isolated communities. This commingling of ideas and assets affected many aspects of Shaker life, including basketry. Sturdy workbaskets that artisans made at South Union, Kentucky, for instance, demonstrate a particularly fascinating mix of influences. Like other Appalachian baskets, those from South Union are made of white oak splint rather than the ash used by other Shakers. Their forms, however, clearly resemble those developed in the earlier-settled northern Shaker community of Mount Lebanon in New York, indicating commerce of some sort between north and south. Elder Daniel Boler, who oversaw basketmaking operations at Mount Lebanon for many years, was a member of the South Union family as a boy, and may have assisted its basketmakers in later years.

Beginning early in the 1800s, the Shakers began to sell many of their high-quality products, including seeds, brooms, oval boxes, chairs, and baskets. The hub of the commercial Shaker basketmaking industry was at Mount Lebanon, where the sect's central ministry presided, and several senior leaders practiced and championed the craft. The Mount Lebanon community's basketmaking industry, which first offered baskets for sale in 1809, was extraordinarily productive. Demand for the Shakers' clearly superior products grew quickly, and Daniel Boler ensured that Mount Lebanon's basketmaking capability kept pace with the retail opportunity. Several hundred baskets were produced annually as early as the 1840s, and surviving records of this thriving commercial enterprise reveal that between 1855 and 1874, when Boler oversaw operations, Mount Lebanon's basketmakers averaged over three thousand baskets a year.

At first, the Mount Lebanon Shakers produced only sturdy but elegant workbaskets, primarily intended for hard outdoor use. In later years, however, most of the community's basketmakers were women, who produced fancy baskets, intended for indoor use as sewing baskets, containers for personal items, or decorative souvenirs of a visit to the village. These delicate baskets, which were often made with extremely fine splint, have been named for their forms or weaving styles. Catheads and their tiny, purely dec-

orative little sisters, called kittenheads, for example, rest on four outside points and resemble a cat's profile. Twilled baskets have round bases intricately woven with a unique Shaker pattern that resembles a four-leaf clover.

Interest in the Shaker religion began to decline after the Civil War. The profound societal changes wrought by the war and the growth of industrial capitalism made the Shakers' simple, methodical, agricultural way of life seem increasingly quaint and outdated. Formerly prosperous villages suffered economically because the meticulous, time-consuming approach of Shaker industries could not compete with an increasing supply of inexpensive factory-made goods. Because they were celibate, the Shakers depended entirely on converts to perpetuate their faith. As the century wore on, fewer new people came to the villages, elderly Shakers died, and many recent converts left to try other, less demanding (or more promising) ways of life. By the dawn of the twentieth century only about

above: TWILLED BASKETS AND TABLE MAT

Unknown Shaker Sisters. c. 1880. New Lebanon, New York. Ash. Largest diameter: 11"; smallest diameter: 4¾". The Shaker Museum, Old Chatham, New York, and Fruitlands Museum, Harvard, Massachusetts. Photograph by Paul Rocheleau.

The weave pattern seen here is unique to Shaker fancy work. Shaker twilled baskets were extremely popular with Victorian buyers. At once decorative and practical, the twill pattern allowed Shaker Sisters to craft round bottoms with thin, lightweight splint rather than having to brace the form with heavier material.

a thousand Believers remained, and by the outset of World War II, all but four villages had closed. Today only the community at Sabbathday Lake, Maine, is still inhabited.

Although fewer than a dozen Brothers and Sisters remain at Sabbathday Lake to continue the Shaker way of life, the art of Shaker basketmaking has paradoxically enjoyed a tremendous revival in recent years. As interest in American history, traditional crafts, and artifacts grew in the 1960s and especially after the Bicentennial in 1976, so did interest in the Shakers. The long overlooked Shaker handcrafts, including their furniture, oval boxes, and baskets, came to represent a signal chapter of American design, and their value skyrocketed. Beginning in the early 1970s, several young museum curators, craftspeople, and scholars began to reexamine the historical record of Shaker life and craftsmanship. Throughout the past two decades, these individuals have identified and elucidated many techniques of Shaker basketmaking and other crafts, and their efforts have, in turn, helped bring the excellence of Shaker work to broad public and critical attention. In 1986, June Sprigg, who was then the curator of Hancock Shaker Village, organized an exhibition of Shaker design at the Whitney Museum of American Art in New York City. This exhibition marked the first time a museum had presented Shaker handcrafts as works of art, thus firmly establishing the artistic importance of Shaker artifacts. Along with outstanding Shaker museums like the ones at Hancock, Massachusetts; Canterbury, New Hampshire; Old Chatham, New York; and Pleasant Hill, Kentucky, dozens of other major public institutions now give Shaker rooms or artifacts a prominent place among their exhibits of American decorative arts. They include the Metropolitan Museum of Art in New York, the Museum of Fine Arts in Boston, the Philadelphia Museum of Fine Art, the M. H. de Young Museum in San Francisco, and the Henry Francis Du Pont Winterthur Museum in Delaware.

opposite: GROUP OF SHAKER WORK BASKETS
Artists unknown. c. 1880. New Lebanon, New York; Canterbury, New Hampshire; and Sabbathday Lake, Maine. Black ash, hardwood handles. Collection of Richard Klank. Photograph by Paul Rocheleau.
Note the openwork cheese basket in the foreground. Like other farmers in the Northeast, Shakers made many such hexagonal weave baskets.

below: WORK BASKETS
Unknown Shaker Brothers. c. 1860. South Union, Kentucky. White oak. Shaker Museum at South Union, South Union, Kentucky. Photograph by Shutterbug, Bowling Green, Kentucky.
Marked "O.F." and "N.F." for "Office Family" and "North Family," these two work baskets are typical of the white oak work baskets made in this southern Shaker community. They represent a distinctive mingling of Shaker and Appalachian basketmaking traditions.

above: RECTANGULAR AND
ROUND WORK BASKETS
Unknown Shaker artists. Left: c. 1865. Community unknown. Black ash, hickory handles, copper tacks. 17¼" x 18⅜" x 14". Right: c. 1840–1870. Mount Lebanon, New York. Black ash, white ash, hickory handle, copper tacks. 16" x 15¼" x 13½". Hancock Shaker Village, Hancock, Massachusetts. Photograph by Paul Rocheleau.
The always practical Shakers used rust-resistant copper tacks to attach supports to the bottoms of their work baskets.

opposite: CROCHET BASKET
John McGuire. 1998. Geneva, New York. Black ash splint, heartwood of hickory, silver eyelet. OH: 11", D: 5½". Private collection.
McGuire worked as the first resident basketmaker for Hancock Shaker Village and has written a book about traditional Shaker basketry. This fancy basket is a reproduction of a classic nineteenth-century Shaker form designed to hold yarn or thread. The top and bottom feature an open hexagonal weave similar to that used in cheese baskets. The handle is inserted and folded back to prevent removal.

The dominant figure in the revival of interest in Shaker basketmaking has been Martha Wetherbee, who, with her partner Nathan Taylor, first encountered Shaker baskets in the mid-1970s. Wetherbee and Taylor were so struck by the baskets and the people who had made them that they decided to learn the craft themselves. At that time two Shaker communities existed, so they befriended a number of the Elders and researched the art of basketmaking. Since none of the remaining Shakers were basketmakers, Wetherbee and Taylor worked backward, studying the surviving Shaker baskets in order to understand how they had been made. Wetherbee's work has inspired hundreds of people around the country and has helped to spread interest in Shaker basketmaking.

A number of other basketmakers, especially in New England, make Shaker-influenced baskets. One extremely talented artisan currently working in traditional Shaker style is Gerrie Kennedy, who has been the resident basketmaker at Hancock Shaker Village in Massachusetts since 1988. Kennedy specializes in the difficult and time-consuming fancy baskets that the Shakers sold to tourists in the later years. She crafts delicate cathead and kittenhead forms in a variety of sizes, fancy Shaker sewing and knife baskets, and circular baskets and mats with twill-woven quatrefoil bottoms.

Ann Lee predicted that when the number of surviving Shakers could be counted on a child's hand, a great revival would take place and converts would flock to the faith. Although the religious revival she envisioned has not yet happened, there is more interest in the Shakers than ever before in history, and at least their way of life will survive through the artifacts created by the craftspeople. The extraordinary baskets that the Shakers created continue to speak eloquently of the people who crafted them and challenge present-day admirers to live as gracefully as the Shakers did.

The Taconic Area

above and left:
MARKET BASKET (DETAIL)
Artist unknown. c. 1880. West Taghkanic, New York, area. White oak splint, hickory rim and handle, black ash lashings. Overall height: 13", W: 10½", L: 15½". Private collection.
A typically sturdy and well-made Taconic utility basket, ideal for carrying goods to and from the store or market.

opposite: ASSEMBLED NEST OF ROUND BASKETS
Artists unknown. c. 1850–1880. West Taghkanic, New York, area. White oak splint, black ash lashings, hickory rims and handles. Height of largest basket: 11". Collection of Nellie Ptasvek. Photograph by Ken Burris.
Taconic basketmakers crafted round utilitarian baskets in a variety of sizes. Their largest baskets were made with paired eared handles, which distributed the weight of heavy loads evenly and allowed a full basket to be carried by two people if necessary.

The quality of surviving Shaker basketry is so consistently high and its appeal to collectors is so strong that many people label every well-made northeastern splint basket as "Shaker" or "possibly Shaker." This

above: SWING-HANDLED BASKETS

Artists unknown. c. 1850–1880. West Taghkanic, New York, area. White oak splint, black ash lashings, hickory handles and rims. Left: Overall height: 12", D: 10"; center: H: 7", D: 12", bottom: 10" square; right: L: 15", overall height: 14½", W: 9½". Collection of Nellie Ptasvek. Photograph by Ken Burris.

Taconic basketmakers were renowned for their high quality swing-handled baskets, the great majority of which were round. The rare rectangular basket at right was used as an asparagus gathering basket; its unusually high handle left plenty of room for the picker to tuck tall stalks"

is due in large part to the increased monetary value attached to such an attribution. In recent years, however, students and practitioners of traditional northeastern basketry have succeeded in distinguishing true Shaker-made pieces from similar baskets. At the same time, they have directed much deserved attention to neglected or misattributed work by other talented artisans in the region. By far the most important of these historic clarifications has involved Taconic basketry. For many years historians misidentified as Shaker the work of skilled professional basketmakers in the Taconic region of Columbia County, New York. Today Taconic basket-making is gaining recognition as a distinct tradition in its own right, and properly identified Taconic baskets now bring solid prices based on their own merits.

Immigrants from the Palatinate, a district of southwest Germany located west of the Rhine, came to America just before the Revolutionary

War and settled in the rich farmlands along the east bank of the Hudson River, southeast of Albany, New York. These newcomers began the Taconic basketmaking tradition. Like many other German immigrants, they formed tight-knit communities, the center of which, in this case, came to be called Germantown. When the Revolution erupted, these recent immigrants, who sided with the Loyalists but wished to avoid conflict, abandoned their homes and hid in the wooded hills where they lived in simple shacks, safe from both the patriots and British soldiers.

The earliest surviving Taconic baskets date from the mid-1700s, not long after settlement, so the German immigrants undoubtedly brought some knowledge of basketmaking from Europe. They also must have learned from Native American artisans in the region, who may have introduced them to splint basketry. Surrounded by good basketmaking timber in their adopted woodland homes, many of the Germans began splint basketmaking as a means of supporting themselves.

During the nineteenth and early twentieth centuries, forty to fifty families, centered in the town of West Taghkanic, New York, practiced basketry. The Shakers at the nearby settlements of Mount Lebanon, New York, and Hancock, Massachusetts, apparently knew and admired Taconic work: both Shaker communities used Taconic baskets in addition to their own. Some experts speculate that the Shakers found it more convenient to buy the swing-handled baskets made by Taconic artisans than to try to improve upon them.[13]

Taconic basketmakers were just as skilled as their Shaker neighbors, but their approaches and techniques differed in several ways. Careful inspection of materials and forms will usually separate Taconic from Shaker work. Unlike most other northeastern craftspeople, Taconic basketmakers were not strict devotees of ash, for example; they used oak and hickory in their work as well. As a result, the presence of a mixture of woods virtually guarantees that a bas-

below: **CHURCH COLLECTION PLATE**
Artist unknown. c. 1850–1880. West Taghkanic, New York, area. White oak splint, black ash lashings, hickory rim. H: 2¾", D: 11¼". Collection of Nellie Ptasvek. Photograph by Ken Burris.
Used to collect offerings in a local church, this is the only known Taconic basket in this form.

following pages: **ROUND WORK BASKETS AND MINIATURES**
Artists unknown. c. 1850–1920. West Taghkanic, New York, area. White oak splint, black ash lashings, hickory handles and rims. Height of largest basket: 11", overall height of smallest: ¾". Collection of Nellie Ptasvek. Photograph by Ken Burris.
Miniatures were popular with tourists, who appreciated both their novel sizes and correspondingly small and affordable prices. Even the tiniest Taconic miniatures followed the simple utilitarian forms of full-size baskets.

137

above: TACONIC FRIENDSHIP
BASKETS

*Left and center by Frank Hotaling; right: artist
unknown. c. 1900–1920. West Taghkanic, New
York. Left and center: maple; right: oak, ash and
hickory. Left: overall height: 8½", D: 11"; center:
overall height: 4½", D: 5½"; right: overall height:
7", D: 7½", bottom: 6½" square. Collection of
Nellie Ptasvek. Photograph by Ken Burris.*
According to Taconic basket historian
Nellie Ptasvek, Frank Hotaling occasionally did odd jobs for an elderly woman in
town, who, in addition to paying him for
his work, also usually insisted on serving
him a home-cooked meal. To even the
score, Hotaling often brought a little
friendship basket with him and gave it to
his benefactor after dinner as a token of
his appreciation for her cooking.

ket is Taconic. Typically the Taconic craftspeople employed oak splint with
a hickory rim and handles and black ash lashings around the rim. Shaker
basket rims are also invariably single-lashed, unlike the rims of Taconic
baskets which are always double-lashed, with the second row of lashing
crossing over the first to create a series of X's.

Taconic basketmakers concentrated almost exclusively on utilitarian
forms such as eared and swing-handled workbaskets, cribs, and fishing
creels. In later years, to satisfy the tourists' demand for souvenirs and to test
the skills of their artisans, Taconic craftspeople often made miniature versions of their full-size forms, the tiniest of which are smaller than a thim-
ble and are said to have been woven with a needle. While extremely well
made, Taconic baskets are generally more utilitarian in appearance than
those of the Shakers. Taconic basket forms tend to be sturdier and some-
what less refined, and they use thicker splint of a uniform size. The Shakers

made many rectangular forms, and some round Shaker baskets made at Mount Lebanon have square bottoms. By contrast, Taconic basketmakers concentrated mainly on round baskets, most of which have round bases. The few Taconic baskets that combine a square base with a round top lack the graceful flow of the Mount Lebanon Shakers' blending of these shapes.

The daintiest of Taconic baskets, and the only Taconic works that rival the airy delicacy of the Shakers' late nineteenth-century fancy baskets are their so-called friendship baskets. Used to carry cookies on a visit to a neighbor, or to hold sewing materials, friendship baskets usually have a round base with a raised center, low sides, and split handles. A few square-bottomed friendship baskets were made, but the round form is far more common as well as more elegant.

Like other professional basketmakers around the Northeast, Taconic artisans found that demand for their work declined drastically during World War I, and by the end of World War II, only a handful continued the craft. The last descendant of the basketmaking families of West Taghkanic, Elizabeth Proper, single-handedly kept the tradition alive until she lost her sight in the 1980s. Her death marked the end of the long line of Taconic basketmakers, although a number of young northeastern revivalist basketmakers, including Jonathan Kline, John McGuire, Martha Wetherbee, and Stephen Zeh, have been strongly influenced by the Taconic tradition and can produce superb reproductions.

below: ROUND SWING-HANDLED BASKET
John McGuire. 1998. Geneva, New York. Black ash splint, white oak. OH: 13", D: 9". Private collection.
John McGuire established a basketmaking program for Old Sturbridge Village and has served as a consultant to the Farmers Museum in Cooperstown, New York. This New England/New York style basket was inspired by a nineteenth-century form in McGuire's collection. Like traditional Taconic baskets, it features a mixture of woods and a double-lashed rim. McGuire says he feels that basketmaking is a contradictory art, that "assures continuity and defies predicability . . . adds a serenity and ignites our passion." He defines a traditional basket as "a vessel that serves the ultimate vessel or 'self' rooted in a purity of design and sacredness of function."

Nantucket

above: PURSE BASKET
Susan Chase Ottison; ivory carving by Susan Chase. 1973. Nantucket, Massachusetts. Rattan, oak, ivory. H: 6¾". Collection of Karl and Susan Ottison. Photograph by Jack Weinhold.
A masterful contemporary purse basket, which honors the tradition begun by José Formoso Reyes.

left: NANTUCKET BASKETMAKER CLINTON MITCHELL "MITCHY" RAY shaving staves with a draw knife in his shop, c. 1950.
Nantucket Historical Association, Nantucket, Massachusetts.

opposite: COVERED BASKET WITH HANDLE
Artist unknown. c. 1880. Nantucket, Massachusetts. Rattan, hardwoods. H: 8", D: 12½". Nantucket Historical Association, Nantucket, Massachusetts.
The top of this skillfully made basket is hinged and fitted precisely inside the unlashed top rim.

Located thirty miles off the south coast of Cape Cod, the island of Nantucket possesses a unique identity, which its geographical isolation has always protected. Nantucket's original settlers, the Wampanoag Indians, gave it the name meaning

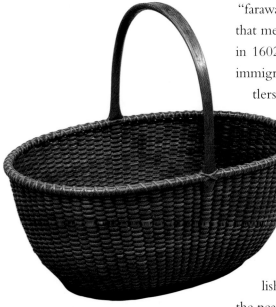

above: OVAL BASKET WITH FIXED HANDLE

Artist unknown. c. 1880. New South Shoal lightship, Nantucket, Massachusetts. Rattan, hardwood. Maximum diameter: 13¾". Collection of Paul and Diane Madden. Photograph courtesy of Hugh Lauter Levin Associates, Southport, Connecticut.

Nantucket baskets with fixed handles are extremely rare, and the combination of the uncommon oval form with a fixed handle makes this lightship basket a double rarity.

"faraway island," or "land far away at sea." The island, an oversized sandbar that measures only 3½ by 14 miles, was discovered by European explorers in 1602. Approximately 1,500 Indians lived on the island when English immigrants first arrived in the mid–seventeenth century; these early settlers were mostly Quakers, whose pious, quietly forbearing, no-nonsense approach to life helped to establish Nantucket's distinctive character.

In 1712, Nantucket captain Christopher Hussey became the first islander to kill a sperm whale, thereby launching an American whaling industry that soon dominated the island's economy and made it the center of the whaling world for many years. By midcentury, Nantucket whalers were sailing throughout the Atlantic in search of the mammal and had established a steady, direct commerce between Nantucket and London. At the peak of the whaling trade in the early nineteenth century, the town of Nantucket was the third largest city in Massachusetts, outranked only by Boston and Salem; over eighty whaling ships sailed out of Nantucket harbor on three- to five-year voyages that took them around the world.

Nantucket basketmaking, which probably began in the 1840s, just as the whaling industry began to decline, is an outgrowth of the extensive coopering industry on the island. The principal product of the whaling industry was, of course, oil, which was used to fuel lamps throughout Europe and America. That oil was stored and shipped in oak barrels made by a host of skilled coopers. These coopers undoubtedly made the first Nantucket baskets as well, transferring some of the trade's techniques, forms, and terms—"staves" for ribs, "hoops" for rims, "bails" for handles—to the craft of basketmaking.

Like the buckets and barrels they resemble, early Nantucket baskets were sturdy and functional. Although many of the island's present-day baskets are purely decorative, Nantucket baskets were originally designed for hard everyday use. Artisans built them, like barrels, around circular or occasionally oval bases of riven oak. They created a groove around the outside edge of the base into which they could insert thin upright ribs, or staves, to form the sides of the basket. Basketmakers closely spaced these staves, which were made of oak, ash, or hickory, to provide a tight structure; a typical Nantucket basket has from forty to eighty staves. A lashed, hooped

rim, again like the rim of a barrel, finished the basket form and held the ribs in place at the top. Tiny copper, iron, or brass nails secured the staves to the rim.

Weavers shaped their baskets around carved wooden molds or forms using imported rattan. Whalers first brought rattan to Nantucket after encountering it during their voyages to the tropical Pacific, where it was cheap, plentiful, and readily available. Rattan, which comes from the stems of climbing tropical palms of the genus *Calamus,* provides a narrow, delicate-looking material that, contrary to its appearance, is extremely strong and pliant. Because it allowed Nantucket basketmakers to achieve an extremely thin and tight weave structure, rattan quickly became the signature material of Nantucket craftspeople.

Although the bails, or handles, of some Nantucket baskets are stationary and a few baskets have no handles at all, the majority of Nantucket baskets have swing handles. Basketmakers attached these handles to ears at either side of the basket rim so they would lie flat against the top when the basket was not in use. They carefully carved the handles from hardwood,

above: GROUP OF NANTUCKET BASKETS

Artists unknown except right front by George Washington Ray. c. 1875. Nantucket, Massachusetts. Rattan, various hardwoods. Diameter of smallest basket: 8½". Collection of Paul and Diane Madden. Photograph courtesy Hugh Lauter Levin Associates, Southport, Connecticut.

An assemblage of vintage Nantucket "lightship" baskets, showing the range of sizes and styles offered by late nineteenth-century island craftsmen.

opposite: SWING-HANDLED
BASKET

Frederick Ray. c. 1890. Nantucket, Massachusetts. Rattan, hardwoods. H: 5¼", D: 9¼". Nantucket Historical Association, Nantucket, Massachusetts. Although Frederick Ray was undoubtedly a member of the extended and prolific Ray family of basketmakers, his life dates and exact relationship remain elusive. This basket was made aboard the *Cross Rip,* a lightship that stood much nearer shore than the better-known *New South Shoal.*

producing delicate, deceptively strong, and beautifully shaped accents to complement the baskets they topped. Typically, the artisans bowed the handles in sweeping arcs to mirror the shape of the basket. Early baskets had handles made from green wood, which their makers bent and tied into shape, while modern Nantucket basket handles are steamed and molded into shape. A few Nantucket baskets also have lids, which, like the baskets themselves, are woven with rattan around a hardwood center and a ribbed frame.

During whaling days, artisans sometimes lashed the rims of Nantucket baskets with baleen, taken from the keratinous plates with which right whales strain tiny krill shrimp from the sea. The whalers processed the strong but extremely flexible baleen for a variety of uses, ranging from corset stays to umbrella ribs. Many early Nantucket-made shorebird decoys have bills fashioned from baleen, and a few basketmakers used the dark gray baleen as weavers to contrast boldly with light brown rattan.

Nantucket baskets were sometimes graduated in size so that they fit one inside the other, the use of molds making the precise sizing possible. Constructing these sets, most of which contained three to eight baskets, was a challenge, but the basketmakers' customers found the nests irresistible. Although nested baskets are usually round, a few oval nests do exist. The introduction of the technically difficult oval form is attributed to master craftsman Davis Hall, and the choicest early oval nests are believed to be his work.

As whaling declined during the second half of the nineteenth century, Nantucketers increasingly looked to other means of making a living. A number of skilled people turned to handcrafts, including basketmaking. During this period, keepers aboard the lightship *New South Shoal* largely established the Nantucket basket tradition. Lightships served locations where lighthouses could not be built. In 1856 the *New South Shoal* was first anchored nineteen miles southwest of Nantucket at the outside approach to a treacherous area of shallow water and shifting sandbars.

Like whaling, lightship keeping was a tedious occupation, filled with seemingly endless hours of leisure, isolation, and discomfort. Keepers aboard the ship found that basketmaking helped pass the time and also provided a few extra dollars to supplement their wages. Most of the ten or twelve crewmen were Nantucketers, and most of them made baskets.

preceding pages: PURSE BASKETS
José Formoso Reyes. c. 1950–1956. Nantucket, Massachusetts. Rattan, oak, ivory. H: 6¾". Private collection. Photograph by Jack Weinhold.
Three fine examples of José Reyes's trademark rattan-staved "friendship" baskets. The scrimshawed ivory on two of the baskets is by Aletha Macy, while the third was carved by Nancy Chase. All three baskets have Reyes's signature and an outline map of Nantucket burnt into their oak bottoms.

below: NANTUCKET BASKET-MAKER JOSÉ FORMOSO REYES at work in his shop, c. 1960. Reyes caught at work on a utilitarian basket. He is beginning to weave rattan through the wooden staves, which he has set in place over a mold. Note the signature friendship purse baskets at his left and hanging above his head.
Nantucket Historical Association, Davidson Collection, Nantucket, Massachusetts.

Some of these men, like Andrew J. Sandsbury, served twenty or more years aboard the ship and made baskets throughout their tour of duty.

By the 1870s lightship basketmakers were advertising their wares in the island's newspaper, and "rattan" or "lightship baskets," as they were soon known, became popular souvenirs among the increasing number of summer visitors. Shop owners also offered lightship baskets, which became an emblem of the island. An 1879 ad in the island's *Inquirer and Mirror* read, "Mrs. Geo. R. Folger offers for sale at the store directly opposite the Pacific Bank . . . a splendid assortment of curiosities, moss and shell work, sea shells, homemade fancy articles, old crockery and a large assortment of rattan baskets made on board the South Shoals [*sic*] Lightship. The public are invited to call and examine."[14] Islanders found the durable baskets adaptable to a variety of purposes; costing about a dollar and lasting for generations, they became ubiquitous in the homes of Nantucketers.

Professional Nantucket basketmakers and sellers sometimes signed or labeled their work, unlike craftsmen in other traditions; as a result, the work of a particular hand can be identified. The flat wooden bottoms of the baskets provided an ideal location for a signature or paper label, and many makers recognized the economic value of identifying their products as lightship baskets or, in later years, simply as Nantucket-made. Today the marks of such outstanding craftsmen as Andrew Sandsbury, Davis Hall, Captain James Wyer, and Charles B. Ray can add significantly to a basket's value.

Basketmaking aboard the lightship came to an end in the 1890s. The *New South Shoal* was blown off its mooring a final time in 1892, and although other ships replaced it, they were increasingly staffed with off-islanders who were not interested in making the lightship baskets that epitomize the Nantucket tradition. Many fine baskets have been made in the hundred years since the *New South Shoal*'s final bout with the weather, however, and many baskets were also made on the island both during and after the lightship years.

By the 1930s, however, a handful of makers were keeping the craft alive. By far the most important of these was Clinton Mitchell "Mitchy" Ray, whose father and grand-father had also been basketmakers. Ray continued to make baskets through the 1940s; by then he was almost single-handedly maintaining the tradition and planning for its future. After World War II, Ray taught the craft to a Harvard-educated Filipino named José Formoso Reyes.

By coincidence or destiny, Reyes had worked with rattan while living in the Philippines and had supplemented his income by repairing cane and rush chair seats, so rattan basketry was a logical next step. In the late 1940s, Reyes introduced a new form of Nantucket basket, a covered lady's handbag that he called a friendship basket. These baskets, made with rattan ribs and covers to which Reyes added decorative carved ivory or ebony, are now the most familiar and often replicated Nantucket basket form. Reyes continued to make baskets until his death in 1980. By that time interest in Nantucket baskets was widespread, with fine antique examples sometimes bringing in hundreds of dollars apiece.

Nantucket lightship baskets remain among the best loved of all American baskets, and their future, especially as decorative items, seems assured by the many makers who continue to practice and refine the art. Today's baskets differ from traditional baskets in their strong emphasis on decorative elements that were introduced by José Reyes. Many carry elaborate scrimshaw carvings of whales, sailboats, shells, or seabirds, while others have handles or covers embellished with etchings of flowers, lighthouses, and other Nantucket scenes. Like Reyes's baskets, the carvings and etchings are often personalized to suit the customer's desires and can include a monogram or a picture with a special meaning. Today's artisans have also expanded their range to include miniatures, cradles, ice buckets, picnic baskets, and other nontraditional forms. Contemporary Nantucket baskets are available in many shops on the island, just as they were a hundred years ago. Whether old or new, traditional or nontraditional, the lightship basket continues to epitomize the Nantucket experience for visitors who want to take home a piece of the island and its history.

above: OVAL BASKET WITH SWING HANDLE
Clinton Mitchell Ray. c. 1920. Nantucket, Massachusetts. Rattan, beechwood, oak. H: 4", L: 10", W: 7½". Private collection. Photograph by Jack Weinhold.
A fine example of Mitchell Ray's early utilitarian work. A printed label reading "Made by/Mitchell Ray/Nantucket, Mass" is attached to the basket's bottom.

following page: NEST OF EIGHT ROUND SWING-HANDLED BASKETS
Davis Hall. c. 1895. Nantucket, Massachusetts. Rattan, hardwoods. Diameter of largest basket: 13"; smallest basket: 4¾". Nantucket Historical Association, Nantucket, Massachusetts.
Davis Hall (1828–1905) served on the *New South Shoal* lightship under Captain Andrew Stansbury from 1882–1891. This nest was made for Ida Cummings Prescott of New Bedford, Massachusetts, whose name is inscribed on each of the handles. She married Dr. Charles Dudley Prescott in 1895, and this set may have been commissioned by him as a wedding gift.

Collecting

ANTIQUE Nantucket baskets are among the most coveted and valuable of all American baskets, and prices for choice examples have risen steadily over the years. Outstanding baskets can earn a few thousand dollars, depending on size, rarity, provenance, and condition. A set of six nested baskets made by Davis Hall set the record at an astonishing $118,000, or nearly $20,000 apiece, in January 1994, when Sotheby's auctioned off the legendary Nina and Bertram Little collection. That price was undoubtedly something of an aberration, at least partially attributable to a virulent case of auction fever, but several other high-quality nested sets have brought substantial five-figure prices.

The most important element affecting the value of a Nantucket basket is patina. Light-colored rattan darkens considerably with time, ideally aging to a rich nut-brown color. The most pleasing baskets have a soft, warm appearance, with the variegated color of the tightly spaced weavers creating subtle, rhythmic patterns of light and dark accents that perfectly complement the spare, graceful lines of the basket's form. A few Nantucket baskets were painted, and a finely crafted basket sporting a well-worn coat of paint is a real find.

Oval forms, high-sided baskets, delicate miniatures, and baskets with flared rims or double handles are highly coveted rare forms. Mitchell Ray and his contemporary Sherman Boyer made a number of tiny "one egg"–size baskets especially for island tourists, and these little baskets make a delightful complement to full-size examples of similar form and construction. While swing handles are the norm for lightship baskets, larger, open baskets typically have low pairs of eared side handles. These fixed-handle examples are quite rare and can command a premium.

Historian David Wood has identified the work of about seventy different Nantucket craftsmen.[15] Since labeled or signed baskets by documented makers are uncommon, this verification is particularly desirable. The paper labels,

brands, and signatures attached to the insides or bottoms of baskets by some craftsmen and agents add a sense of history to a basket and provide a firm link to the maker. Paper labels are fragile and easily damaged, though, so the more complete the label or signature, the better. In addition to the basket-makers mentioned above, William D. Appleton, Oliver Coffin, George Folger, George Washington Ray, Ferdinand Sylvaro, and A. D. Williams rank among the most accomplished of Nantucket's identified craftsmen.

above: OPEN ROUND BASKET WITH INSET SIDE HANDLES
Artist unknown. c. 1880. Nantucket, Massachusetts. Rattan, hardwoods. H: 4¼", D: 9½". Nantucket Historical Association, Nantucket, Massachusetts.
Note the grooved handles, which are carefully carved to provide a firm, comfortable hand grip.

The Pennsylvania Dutch and Other Germans

Beginning in colonial days and continuing through the nineteenth century, immigrants from the German-speaking areas of Europe, including Silesia, Alsace, Moravia, Switzerland, and the Rhineland itself, came to America, bringing their strong

opposite: COVERED STORAGE BASKET
Artist unknown. c. 1830–1850. North or South Carolina. Rye straw, white oak splint. 28" x 40" x 33". High Museum of Art, Atlanta, Georgia. Purchased with funds from the Decorative Arts Acquisition Trust, 1993.12.
The strands of rye that make up the coil bundles can be seen in the broken coils at the top and bottom of this well-used old Carolina basket.

below: PENNSYLVANIA RYE STRAW BASKETMAKER MARIE STOTLER at work.

religious and cultural traditions with them. Often they settled together, most notably in Pennsylvania, where Lutherans, German Reformed, Amish, Mennonites, Schwenkfelders, Moravians, German-speaking Huguenots, and other Deutsch (hence the English corruption "Dutch") Protestants took advantage of William Penn's "holy experiment," the promises of religious freedom and free land. Smaller numbers of these immigrants also settled in parts of Virginia, Tennessee, and North Carolina, where their language and distinctive cultural and craft traditions set them apart from their neighbors, who were primarily of British or Scots-Irish descent.

Primarily farmers who came from some of the richest agricultural lands in Europe, the Deutsch tended to settle areas of equal or greater richness in America, especially the immensely fertile land of southeastern Pennsylvania. This was no coincidence; William Penn, who had toured the Rhineland in 1677, "knew firsthand about the excellent farming practices there. He saw war-ruined farms and discontented farmers and craftsmen, and he made inviting offers . . . to stimulate their removal to Pennsylvania."[16] Once in America, the industrious Germans set immediately to work, establishing highly efficient and productive farms that typically combined field crops, orchards, house gardens, and livestock and involved all members of the extended family, old and young alike, in a daily round of hard work.

While the German immigrants who settled in Pennsylvania and other mid-Atlantic and southern states greatly contributed to America's artistic tradition with their sgrafitto-decorated redware pottery, calligraphic fraktur birth and baptismal records, and highly stylized carved or paint-decorated furniture, their baskets also remain demonstrably different from those of any other cultural or regional group in the country. Like their pottery, paintings, and furniture, the baskets strongly reflect long-standing European

above: BASKET TRAY

Artist unknown. c. 1850. Wythe County, Virginia. Rye straw, white oak splint. Collection of Roddy and Sally Moore. Photograph by Ken Burris.
This platelike basket was probably used as a food serving tray.

traditions that continued to be a part of their home and family life in the New World well into the nineteenth century.

The preferred material of traditional German-American basketmakers was rye straw, a staple material of basketmakers throughout Europe but rarely used in the New World except in German immigrant communities. Farmers grew and harvested rye specifically for basketmaking; when they cut off the heads of grain, the long strands of the grass provided a strong and durable but flexible material. Indeed, rye is the strongest and tallest of all the grains; baskets coiled from its six-foot-long strands were tough enough to stand up to the elements and also deter rodents from chewing them. After curing the straw for several months, the basketmakers soaked it in water to make the material more pliable. They then gathered bundles of rye straw into coils, laid them on top of each other in rows, and tied them together with thin splints of oak to form the basket. Depending on the size

of the basket, the coils used to construct it could range in thickness from a pencil width to a full inch. The nature of rye straw construction limited the craftsperson to simple round or oval shapes, but the baskets were structurally very sturdy because of the thickness of the coils, and some rye straw hampers and covered storage baskets were very large. Most rye straw baskets had no handles, but some craftsmen wove handles of straw or carved them from oak or hickory and then attached them to the basket with nails.

Two of the most common German-American rye straw baskets—the beehive, or skep, and the bread-raising basket—are unique to this tradition, while a third, the covered hamper, is uncommon in other traditions. German-Americans were avid gardeners who often kept bees, both for their honey, which they used to sweeten baked goods, and as pollinators of their fruits and vegetables. Apiarists had used skeps made of rye straw throughout Europe for centuries, and immigrants introduced the tradition

above: SPLIT-HANDLED BASKET
Artist unknown. c. 1850. Wythe County, Virginia.
Rye straw and oak splint, oak handle. Collection
of Roddy and Sally Moore. Photograph by Ken
Burris.
An unusual and fairly impractical form.

to America by setting out coiled-straw skeps in which the bees could build hives. Skeps were generally shaped like inverted bowls, a foot and a half to two feet tall, with a small entrance hole at the bottom center of one side. The beekeeper provided a framework for comb-building by inserting a pair of crossed oak sticks into the middle of the skep. He would then either place a queen inside to attract a swarm of bees, or he would simply set the skeps among cultivated herbs and flowers. The thick coils of straw acted as insulation; the straw hives were warmer in winter and cooler in summer than those made of wood or other materials, and they were relatively inexpensive. The apiarists could easily reach the honey combs by turning the skep over. However, because they had to remove the entire comb, farmers had to kill the bees first, lest they starve to death. The introduction of the stackable wooden beehive, which was invented by a Philadelphia clergyman in 1850 and allowed beekeepers to extract both comb and honey a bit at a time without harming their bees, replaced the skep as the preferred apiary tool in America.

Like skeps, rye straw bread-raising baskets came to America with the first German immigrants. These baskets were typically low and open round forms that were sometimes fitted with a cover. After kneading pastry dough, the baker would place it in the basket, cover the bread, then wait for it to rise. Before each use, the baker lined the baskets with cloth, so that the sticky dough would slip out easily. Like bee skeps, bread-raising baskets acted as natural insulators, protecting the fragile yeast from cooling drafts while it acted. The baskets also kept dough clean and dry in the midst of other kitchen activity. While bread-raising baskets rarely had handles, they often had a single coil loop or a series of loops on their sides so they could be hung on the kitchen wall when not in use. German immigrants also used these simple baskets for a host of other household purposes, such as storing nuts, eggs, fruit, herbs, or vegetables and holding balls of yarn, scraps of fabric, and other sewing materials. Larger covered baskets served as storage bins for grains, vegetables, fresh and dried fruits, sheared wool, and feathers gathered for bedding. Heavy, durable baskets stood in cold cellars, sheds, barns, or back rooms, where they served as receptacles for harvested crops.

Rye straw is unfamiliar to most people today. Basket-quality straw is difficult to find, and few contemporary artisans feel the need to make baskets out of this material. An exception is Marie Elena Stotler of Malvern, Pennsylvania, a specialist in skeps who also crafts several different types of bread baskets. An avid herb and flower gardener, she learned the rudiments of straw basketry from a Lancaster Amish couple and then used the techniques to construct a skep for her garden. Stotler was asked by visitors who saw her skep to make one for them, and by sheer chance, she discovered that a neighbor grew rye as bedding for his cows and horses— another traditional use for the crop. Before he cuts and bails his rye, she harvests a year's supply of basketmaking material from his fields, using only a hedge clipper.[17]

below: **BREAD-RAISING BASKET**
Artist unknown. c. 1880. Broadway, Shenandoah County, Virginia. Rye straw, oak splint. 4" x 10½" x 9¾". Collection of Roddy and Sally Moore. Photograph by Ken Burris.
Many German immigrants settled the Shenandoah Valley, moving through southwest Virginia into east Tennessee. Although rye straw baskets have been found in most areas of Virginia that were settled by Germans, openwork baskets like this are rare.

Appalachia

$\mathbf{A}$ppalachia seems almost like a separate country, culturally unified and geographically distinct from the rest of the eastern United States, a place where time has stood still and tradition has reigned. While its boundaries are still debated, Appalachia's

opposite: OVAL BASKET WITH
BAIL HANDLE
*Artist unknown. c. 1900. Virginia. White oak.
Collection of Roddy and Sally Moore. Photograph
by Ken Burris.*
The tall thin handle of this basket was
made to be slung over the user's arm. It
might have been used for gathering flowers or herbs.

geographical core is the so-called Southern Highlands,[18] a vast expanse of
upland rural country that stretches through the Allegheny, Blue Ridge, and
Appalachian mountain chains, encompassing most of West Virginia and
extending south into northwestern Georgia. It is a region of hills and hol-
lows, mountains and woodlands, originally covered by a primarily hardwood forest and crisscrossed by hundreds of rivers, streams, and natural
springs.

The backcountry of Appalachia was settled in the eighteenth century,
primarily by immigrants from Northern Ireland, northern England, and
the Scottish lowlands and islands. The Scots-Irish who populated Appalachia were a fiercely independent group who quickly became and have
remained the dominant cultural group in the region, making up over 90
percent of the population. They brought to America venerable musical and
handcraft traditions as well as rural folkways that are still associated with
Appalachia, including an "extended clan" sense of family, the cabin style of
architecture, and an intensely fatalistic view of life that was born out of
hard experience rather than religious belief.[19]

The rugged terrain made travel within the region difficult and dis-
couraged road building until well into the twentieth century. This isolation
caused the people of Appalachia to remain virtually unchanged during the
tumultuous waves of nineteenth-century immigration. As late as 1910, the
census revealed that less than 1 percent of the population in this region
was foreign-born and nearly 85 percent could trace their origins to the
region's original Scots-Irish settlers.[20]

The way of life within this region continued to be remarkably stable,
thus allowing the transfer of many traditions from generation to generation. In the early years of the twentieth century, for example, the English
folklorist and song collector Cecil Sharp discovered a number of ancient
ballads sung in Appalachia that had vanished from memory in Britain.
Traditional handcrafts also remained relatively unchanged. In 1937 craft
historian Allen Eaton observed,

There is no large area in the United States with such a variety of
handicrafts today as the Southern Highlands, because as a part of
daily life they have persisted longer here than in any other section
of our country. In fact there are places today where life still goes

on in a very primitive way, where plowing is done with oxen, where the family water supply comes from the old spring with the gourd dipper always in reach, where carding and spinning are done by hand and weaving on looms of ancient type, where herbs are gathered for medicine, and barks, roots, and flowers for dyeing yarn, where honey is stored in bee gums made by hollowing out a log, where planting is done according to the light or dark of the moon and where grain is cut with a cradle.[21]

Basketmaking was always an important part of Appalachian life. Well into the twentieth century, baskets were used for countless chores, including gathering eggs, picking berries and nuts, sowing and harvesting vegetables, shearing sheep, feeding domestic animals, storing crops, and carrying goods to and from the market. Both men and women practiced the art of basketmaking; some made baskets strictly for their own use, while other, often more accomplished, artisans who had established local reputations sold or traded baskets to their neighbors. Demand was so strong that many Appalachian storekeepers took baskets in trade for food and supplies, knowing they could easily sell them.

Many highlanders were poor, but their craft kept them from privation. One of Allen Eaton's West Virginia informants, for example, offered the following information about a basketmaker named Levi Eye, who lived in Pendleton County: "Mr. Eye had a family of sixteen, including parents, which he maintained by making and selling baskets. He would barter his baskets for lard, meat, flour, or whatever was needed. I asked him how many baskets he had made in his long lifetime, and he said, 'Well, I was just figuring the other day on the number, and I made it a little over seven thousand. I began when [I was] a small lad, working with my father.'" Several of Eye's sons continued in the trade after their father's death in 1926.[22]

Although Appalachian basketmakers also sometimes used willow, honeysuckle, rye straw, pine needles, raffia, corn husks, and other materials, the primary basketmaking stuff of the region has always been splint prepared from trees of the white oak family. (The edible acorns of white oak, which provide invaluable food for a wide variety of wild animals and birds, distinguish the trees from black and red oaks.) Basketmakers used both the

opposite: OVAL TRAY BASKET WITH SPLIT HANDLE
Artist unknown. c. 1900. Wythe County, Virginia. White oak. H: 12", L: 17". Collection of Roddy and Sally Moore.
This long and rather fragile basket may have been used to hold bread or other food at the table. The unsupported bottom made it suitable only for the lightest of loads.

following pages, left: ROUND BASKET WITH STAINED WEAVERS
Artist unknown. c. 1920. Pulaski County, Virginia. White oak, natural pigments. H: 13½", D: 14¾". Collection of Roddy and Sally Moore. Photograph by Ken Burris.
The stained weavers and stakes are only colored on the outside. The alternating rows of dyed and natural splint create a strong pattern of horizontal color; every other vertical stave is also dyed.

following pages, right: WALL BASKET
Artist unknown. c. 1880. Virginia. White oak. Collection of Roddy and Sally Moore. Photograph by Ken Burris.
As is typical of wall baskets, the back of this example is flat so it would hang flush against the wall.

familiar white oak (*Quercus alba*), and the basket or swamp chestnut oak (*Quercus michauxii*) because their wood was relatively easy to split; however, the adaptable white oak was the more abundant and popular of the two. The basket oak, which is found in bottomlands from central New Jersey south to northern Florida and west into Texas, was much less favored, despite its name.

Appalachian basketmakers sought small unblemished oak trees that would provide the straight-grained wood most suitable for splitting and shaping into basketmaking material. They looked for healthy, upright young trees with trunks about a handspan in diameter and the high branches. Craftsmen would cut the trunk at the lowest branch and bring the clean span of trunk out of the woods before working further. They then stripped off the bark, split the trunk into eight equal sections with an ax or maul, and cut the wood along the grain of the growth rings. They could then halve the pieces across the grain to achieve the desired width, and split them with the grain until they were thin enough to use. The artisans favored heartwood for handles, rims, and ribs and thin, pliable splits of sapwood for weavers. The sapwood weavers, usually only a single ring in thickness, were prepared by hand; a basketmaker would start to divide the wood with a knife, pull a piece carefully in half along its grain, then smooth the piece to a satiny finish with a knife or a piece of glass.

above: CYNTHIA TAYLOR AND AARON YAKIM felling and hauling a carefully chosen white oak tree. Finding quality wood is difficult but absolutely essential to the basketmaking process.

Photograph by Dick Croy.

The region's practical denizens favored ribbed baskets, made by weaving splits through a skeletal rib cage–like framework. Because of their extremely sturdy yet lightweight construction, these baskets could last through years of hard wear. The most recognizable Appalachian basket form is probably the ribbed buttocks basket, so-called for its resemblance to the body part. Craftsmen constructed the bulging form on a foundation of two wide flat hoops, which they set at right angles to create the vertical overhead handle, spine, and horizontal rim of the basket. In order to round off the basket's edges, they often whittled the thin ribs, which extended beyond the edge of the spine to create its unusual shape. To complete the work, the basketmaker wove the ribs with thin, flat splints.

Another ribbed form unique to Appalachia is the Kentucky egg basket, a tall, narrow form originally created to cradle eggs in transit on the back of a horse or mule. Ribbed baskets also exist in rectangular forms with relatively flat bottoms, and some do not have overhead handles. The basketmaker could also leave the rim hoop unwoven for a handspan at either end of the basket to create inset grips.

While ribbed forms epitomize Appalachian basketmaking, many other types of baskets were made in the region. Simple plaited split oak baskets, which are much easier to craft, were probably the region's most common baskets. They existed in a full complement of standard geometric shapes—round, oval, square, and rectangular—to serve a variety of farm and household purposes. Animal feeding and feed storage baskets, workers' lunch pails, sturdy coal-carrying baskets, market baskets, shallow flower-gathering baskets, delicate household trinket and sewing baskets, tall clothes hampers, and even cradles were woven of split oak or, occasionally, hickory, ash, or maple. Oak splint was also sometimes painstakingly whittled or die-cut into cylindrical rods and used to make baskets similar to those made from willow. Widely practiced in the British Isles, the techniques of rod basketry

above and left: MINIATURE RIB BASKET

Possibly by a member of the Mills family. 1983. Eastern Kentucky. Plain and dyed honeysuckle, hickory splint and bark. Overall height: 3¾", D: 3". Collection of Cynthia Taylor. Photograph by Ken Burris.

This little honeysuckle basket was purchased from Red Bird Mission in Beverly, Kentucky, along with a full-size companion by the same unknown hand. This basket's ribs appear to be hickory, while those of the larger basket were made of dogwood. The handle is also hickory and is decoratively wrapped with the inner bark of a hickory tree.

right and opposite: SQUARE-
BOTTOMED BASKET WITH
CROSS-BRACED BOTTOM

*Artist unknown. c. 1900. Craig County, Virginia,
or Monroe County, West Virginia. White oak.
Overall height: 7¼", D: 6½". Collection of Roddy
and Sally Moore. Photograph by Ken Burris.*
This little basket's tightly woven square
bottom is reinforced with disproportion-
ately thick cross braces, giving it the
strength and presence of similarly constructed baskets many times its size.

were undoubtedly brought to Appalachia by the Scots-Irish. The rods,
which were kept moist for pliability, were laced or twisted through a
framework of horizontal side stakes; the most common weave was a simple
one-over, one-under pattern. More complex, twisted weaves employed
groups of two, three, or four rods, which artisans interlaced as they wove
them through the side stakes. Oak rod baskets were even more durable
than those made from oak splits, but relatively few artisans worked with
this material, and therefore the tradition is nearly moribund today.

Some Appalachian artisans wove cut willow rods in a similar fashion.
This wood was not from the familiar weeping willow tree, whose thin
branches break easily, but rather from the basket willow or purple osier
(*Salix purpurea*), a tall shrub introduced from Europe specifically for use in
basketmaking. The basket willow grows up to 25 feet tall and, like other
willows, it favors a damp location, often growing in marshes or along
streams. Basketmakers cut thin young shoots from the willows and either
peeled off the bark or left it intact.

opposite: ROD BASKET
Artist unknown. c. 1880. Virginia. White oak. Collection of Roddy and Sally Moore. Photograph by Ken Burris.
A basket within the skeleton of a basket. The rim and base of this unusual form are connected by an outside framework of single rods.

left and below: ROUND BASKET WITH BYE-STAKED BASE
Ralph Chesney. 1983. Union County, Tennessee. White oak. Overall height: 10", W: 10½", L: 11¼", Diameter of base: 9¼". Collection of Cynthia Taylor. Photograph by Ken Burris.
Chesney is a fastidious craftsman who adds many fine details to his baskets. He carefully carves all the stakes used in the bottom of his round baskets, narrowing the main stakes at the center and then adding many additional sharply pointed bye-stakes alongside to create a unique spoked matrix for his weaving. Also note the added rim at the base and the purely decorative braiding on the handle and both rims. The basket's base is round, while the top is slightly ovoid.

Beginning around the turn of the twentieth century, just as the old ways were starting to fade, a crafts revival began in Appalachia, fostered by missionary educators who imagined it would build local pride, help to preserve important regional traditions, and, perhaps most important, provide much needed work for the area's otherwise unskilled residents. Dozens of craft schools were established throughout the region, including such important and influential centers as Berea College and Arrowmont in Kentucky and Penland in North Carolina. These schools offered training in traditional arts such as quilting, weaving, woodcarving, pottery, and basket-making and, for the first time, marketed Appalachian wares to customers outside the region. Through the efforts of these schools and regional craft centers, a number of which are still active today, the community has maintained a strong, unbroken continuity of traditional craftsmanship.

When Revival-era basketmakers began selling their wares to customers outside the region, they experimented with nonfunctional forms, unusual materials, and decorative techniques. Some of these basketmakers found that the addition of color increased the appeal of their baskets, so they mixed dyed and plain weavers to create alternating rows or patterns of vertical and horizontal color. Others made miniature versions of traditional forms or created small lidded baskets that would find a place on a woman's dressing table. One of the Revival era's best-known basketmakers and teachers was Cordelia Ritchie of Knott County, Kentucky. Working primarily with willow that she had dyed, Ritchie invented her own forms. Her unique three-handled willow Dream Basket, for example, employs traditional workmanship in the creation of an imaginative form that is not based on function. Baskets like Ritchie's exemplify the creative work of Revival artisans because they adapt conservative old traditions to modern sensibilities. This same mixture of individual creativity and respect for tradition continues to enliven Appalachian basketry today.

Appalachia still supports more outstanding traditional basketmakers than any other part of the country. A number of the region's basketmakers, such as Ida Pearl Davis and Thelma Hibdon of Woodbury, Tennessee, continue to work out of long-standing family traditions. Although Davis made baskets throughout her childhood to help support the family, she did not practice the craft again until her retirement from factory work in the early 1970s. For many years after the Great Depression, basketmaking and other traditional handcrafts were viewed as menial lower-class work, so craftspeople like Davis abandoned it. Fortunately, the 1960s saw a renewed respect for traditional handcrafts, and people were encouraged to return to these endeavors. Working with her daughter, Thelma Hibdon, to whom she taught the craft, Ida Pearl Davis produces show baskets that have more numerous ribs and finer splint than traditional utility baskets. The two women employ time-honored methods, making their baskets from materials they have gathered from local woods and painstakingly prepared by hand with drawknives and pocketknives. Davis has recently had to stop making baskets, because of her age and poor health, but Hibdon continues to carry on the family tradition, now with the help of her own daughter, Jennifer Dawn Walls.

Cordelia Everidge ("Aunt Cord") Ritchie. c. 1920. Knott County, Kentucky. Willow dyed with spruce bark. H: 8", D: 13". Southern Highland Craft Guild, Folk Art Center, Asheville, North Carolina. Ritchie said the idea for this fanciful three-handled basket "just came to her" in a dream. The basket is coiled from willow rods.

Other regional artisans like Cynthia Taylor and Aaron Yakim of Parkersburg, West Virginia, were not born into their craft but learned it by studying with older masters. Yakim, who was taught by fifth-generation West Virginia basketmaker Oral Nicholson in the late 1970s, recalls watching Nicholson "head into the woods with only a hatchet in his hand and a knife in his pocket and come out with a basket in hand." Yakim also recalls being powerfully drawn to the "simplicity and functionality of the whole craft."[23] Taylor has carefully observed the work of over thirty traditional

Appalachian artisans since she was introduced to white oak basketry by Rachel Nash Law in 1982. She and Law spent several years researching and documenting traditional Appalachian white oak baskets and basket-makers, and presented their findings in *Appalachian White Oak Basket-making: Handing Down the Tradition,* a scholarly book published by the University of Tennessee Press. Yakim and Taylor have worked in partnership since 1994, producing their own highly refined versions of traditional Appalachian ribbed baskets. In 1998 they were asked to participate in the annual Smithsonian Craft Show, the nation's most prestigious juried exhibition of contemporary crafts.

Still other contemporary basketmakers, like Connie and Tom McColley of Chloe, West Virginia, use time-honored traditional methods to invent new basket forms. The McColleys are artist-craftspeople who call themselves weavers of wood and make distinctive decorative baskets with forms that reflect sophisticated modern design ideas. According to Tom McColley, "We are primarily self-taught, learning by studying old baskets and photographs of baskets. Our earlier work was more traditional in style, basically copies of well-designed traditional white oak baskets. As we gained skill in using the material, we began to push the limits of what had been done before us, expanding the possibilities and redefining our definition of 'basket' in a more contemporary context. Although our baskets deal more with ideas than function, they still maintain a link to the tradition."[24]

opposite: RIBBED HALF-BUSHEL BASKET
Ida Pearl Davis and Thelma Davis Hibdon. 1988. Woodbury, Tennessee. White oak. H: 14½", D: 13¾". Collection of Thelma Davis Hibdon. Photograph by Ken Burris.
An example of the mother and daughter team's many-ribbed show baskets, which they made in a number of different graduated sizes.

following pages: BASKET WITH BRANCH HANDLE
Tom and Connie McColley. 1991. Chloe, West Virginia. White oak, cherry. 16" x 25" x 22". Private collection.
The McColleys often incorporate found materials like this basket's branch handle into their work. This aesthetic reflects the practicality of traditional basketmakers at the same time it is informed by modernist design sensibilities.

Collecting

THE RICH diversity of Appalachian basketry is probably its most appealing feature. It offers collectors an extremely wide range of forms, construction methods, and materials. Collectors can attempt to cover the whole range, or they can specialize in the works of a particular time, such as the nineteenth century, the Revival era, or our own modern period. A collection might also have a central theme—for example, ribbed, split, or rod baskets or those made of unusual materials, such as willow, honeysuckle, corn husks, or long-leaf pine needles. Nineteenth-century Appalachian basketmakers rarely dyed or painted their wares, so early functional examples with these decorative elements are desirable to collectors. An interesting collection could be made of early functional forms juxtaposed with decorative variations on these themes made by Revival-era and modern artisans.

Because historians and collectors have valued, encouraged, and studied the region's handcrafts since the dawn of this century, they have been able to identify many old-time makers. In addition to Cordelia Ritchie, Allen Eaton documented the work of such Revival-era makers as A. O. Burton, Lena and Flora Dysart, Carrie

Lyon, Mac McCarter, Silas Nicholson, Bird Owsley, Nannie B. Sego, Lydia Whaley, and Birdie Willis. All were still active in the mid-1930s, and several sold their work through mountain cooperatives and settlement schools. Owsley, for example, made baskets for the Hindman Settlement School in Kentucky and was best known for his classic high-sided egg baskets. Outstanding traditional artisans of the next generation include Ralph Chesney, Ida Pearl Davis, Dan and Martha Jones, Jessie Jones, Mildred Youngblood, and Lucy and William Cody Cook who demonstrated their craft at Colonial Williamsburg for a number of years. Dozens of other craftspeople continue to produce fine traditional baskets throughout Appalachia; their work is often

available through vibrant cooperatives such as the Southern Highland Handicraft Guild in Asheville, North Carolina. Unlike in many more developed areas of the country, traveling through Appalachia and searching for outstanding contemporary craft work can still be a pleasant and rewarding endeavor.

above: ROUND BASKET WITH EARED HANDLES
Artist unknown. c. 1900. Virginia. White oak. Collection of Roddy and Sally Moore. Photograph by Ken Burris.

opposite: ROD BASKET WITH SCALLOPED BORDER
Artist unknown. c. 1920. Shenandoah Valley, Virginia. White oak. Overall height: 12½", D: top 12". Collection of Larry Hackley. Photograph by Rachel Nash Law and Cynthia Taylor, reproduced courtesy the University of Tennessee Press.
Decorative openwork borders are common in oak and willow rod baskets. The concept was probably brought to America from Europe.

African-Americans of the Southeast Coast

Prior to the Civil War, vast plantations
along the tidewater coasts of South Carolina and Georgia grew almost all of America's rice. The Rice Kingdom, as it was
known, extended north to Wilmington,
North Carolina, and south to Jacksonville,

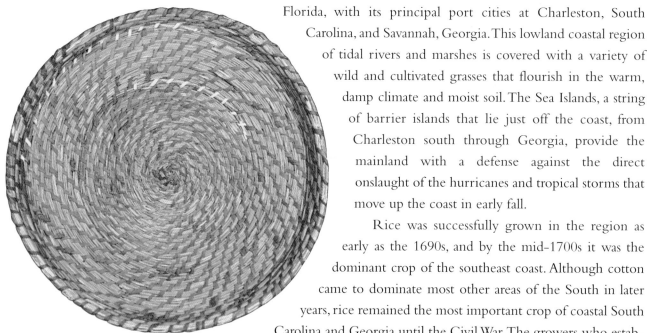

above: RICE FANNER

Artist unknown. c. 1850. South Carolina. Rush and oak. H: 2", D: 20¾". The Charleston Museum, Charleston, South Carolina.

A typical antebellum fanner basket, simple, rugged and perfectly shaped for its specialized function.

opposite: COVERED SEWING BASKET

Florence Mazcyk. 1982. Mount Pleasant, South Carolina. Sweetgrass, rush, pine needles, palmetto leaf. H: 6½", D: 12". McKissick Museum, University of South Carolina, Columbia, South Carolina.

Note the alternating rows of different-colored material and the added strip of decorative coiling on the bottom section. The coils are sewn with light-colored strips of palmetto, which create vertical bands of surface pattern.

Florida, with its principal port cities at Charleston, South Carolina, and Savannah, Georgia. This lowland coastal region of tidal rivers and marshes is covered with a variety of wild and cultivated grasses that flourish in the warm, damp climate and moist soil. The Sea Islands, a string of barrier islands that lie just off the coast, from Charleston south through Georgia, provide the mainland with a defense against the direct onslaught of the hurricanes and tropical storms that move up the coast in early fall.

Rice was successfully grown in the region as early as the 1690s, and by the mid-1700s it was the dominant crop of the southeast coast. Although cotton came to dominate most other areas of the South in later years, rice remained the most important crop of coastal South Carolina and Georgia until the Civil War. The growers who established huge plantations on the mainland and many of the barrier islands became some of the most prosperous of all southern landowners and businessmen.

Because rice was a common crop in coastal West Africa, many plantation owners sought West African slaves who were expert in rice cultivation. The majority of these slaves came to America from the Senegambian region of West Africa between 1750 and 1810. Their experience in rice cultivation made these Africans unique among American slaves and ensured for them an unparalleled social and familial stability. Their skill increased their value to their owners, who needed their knowledge, not simply their brawn, to succeed.

Rice Kingdom slaves introduced many agricultural techniques, including the practice of winnowing threshed rice in large flat circular baskets made from sewn coils of grass. When a worker tossed the rice into the air, the lighter hulls were blown away by the breeze, and the separated rice fell back into the basket. Slaves called the process fanning, for the rhythmic up-and-down motion of the baskets, which came to be known as fanners.

Fanners are still in use in West Africa, and modern examples are virtually identical to those from antebellum rice plantations. The slaves made fanners from coils of bulrush (*Juncus roemericanus*), a tough, thick, and

durable grass that still grows wild in the tidewater marshes of the region. Rush—or rushel, as it was often called locally—was an ideal material for use in fanners and other farm baskets because it was both sturdy and lightweight. Although some slave women made work-baskets, most rush baskets were made by men, whose field-hardened hands could work the tough stems of the grass more efficiently. To make a fanner, basketmakers cut and bundled rush stems together into tightly packed finger-thick rows. They bound the tight bundles of rush with thin strips of oak splint, sewing around each row at regular intervals. A typical fanner measured about two feet in diameter but was only a couple of inches deep, with a wide, flat center and a narrow, splayed outside lip. Slaves also crafted coiled rush storage baskets for the rice. These were similar in diameter to fanners but had straight sides that could measure up to a foot tall. Storage baskets often included a cover as

well. Both fanners and storage baskets were rugged utilitarian objects, made to last through years of hard use in the rice fields. The most common rush baskets created for indoor use were smaller fanner-shaped pieces used as church collection baskets.

The Civil War effectively destroyed the economy that had supported the Rice Kingdom, and the surviving large plantations could not be maintained without inexpensive slave labor. During Reconstruction, most of the plantations were divided into smaller parcels or turned to different uses, leaving thousands of former slaves to look for work in other regions. During and after the Civil War, however, a unique black culture survived on the coastal barrier islands. Union forces captured the islands late in 1861 and freed all the slaves there. Fugitive slaves from many other parts of the South found their way to the islands during the war as well, where they continued to live and farm after the conflict. The remote islands were largely forgotten by the rest of the world until the 1930s, when whites rediscovered them as vacation sites. They found isolated black communities whose people were leading a simple, anachronistic way of life with deep and direct ties to their roots in Africa and the Bahamas, where a

above: COVERED STORAGE BASKET
Artist unknown. c. 1850. Rush sewn with oak splint. Charleston Museum, Charleston, South Carolina.
This simple work basket was made by a slave for plantation use. The white strips on this hard-used old basket are modern conservation repairs, which were purposefully left undisguised.

opposite: THREE-TIERED SEWING BASKET, AND HOT PAD
Left by Mary Jane Manigault, right by Angie Manigault (granddaughter of Mary Jane). 1979. Mount Pleasant, South Carolina. Sweetgrass, palmetto, pine needles. Left: H: 12", D: 11½". Museum of International Folk Art, Santa Fe, New Mexico.
As this assemblage of baskets demonstrates, Mrs. Manigault has successfully passed her artistry on to her descendants. Tiered sewing baskets are made by several Mount Pleasant artisans.

above: MASTER BASKETMAKER
ALFRED GRAHAM teaching a class
at the Penn Normal School, Saint Helena
Island, South Carolina.

*Penn School Historical Collection, Southern
Historical Collection, University of North Carolina
Library, Chapel Hill, reproduced with permission
of the Penn Center, Inc., Saint Helena, South
Carolina.*

number of British Loyalist planters had moved with their slaves during the Revolution. After slavery was abolished in Britain in 1834, those same planters moved back to the United States, this time settling on the Sea Islands, where they assumed slavery would continue.

The Sea Islands retained elements of African and Bahamian culture that had long since disappeared on the mainland, including ring dances, spirituals, and the archaic Gullah language, a unique amalgam of British English (via the Bahamas), American English, and West African dialect. Also among the old folkways preserved on the Sea Islands were rice farming and coiled-grass basketmaking, which had persisted there virtually unchanged throughout the nineteenth century.

When the Penn School on Saint Helena Island, South Carolina, which had been established as a black educational center during Reconstruction, was reorganized in 1904, coiled-seagrass basketmaking was made a part of the curriculum with the intention of giving local blacks the skills they needed to prosper on the islands. A native island basketmaker named Alfred Graham, who had learned basketmaking from his African-born father, taught the craft; shops and customers as far north as Boston successfully sold rush baskets made by Graham and his students. Although interest diminished considerably over the years, basketmaking remained part of the curriculum at the school until 1950, and many students continued to practice and teach the craft elsewhere in the region.

Also in the early years of the twentieth century, several black women in Mount Pleasant, South Carolina, began to sell baskets made of sweetgrass (*Muhlenbergia capillaris* or *M. filipe*) to white customers in the street markets of Charleston. Sweetgrass is much softer and finer than rush, with delicate strands. Since it proved more pliable and versatile than rush, basketmakers could create thinner coils, typically a quarter inch instead of an

Collecting

I N ADDITION to antique examples, traditional New England baskets made by outstanding contemporary craftspeople have become highly collectible in recent years. Work by such talented artisans as Jonathan Kline, John McGuire, Susi Nuss, Joyce Schaum, and Stephen Zeh often equals or surpasses older baskets in its quality and attention to detail; splint baskets by these master craftspeople will undoubtedly become heirlooms in the years to come. Collectors of contemporary work also have the great pleasure of getting to know the people whose work they own, and the joys of these personal connections cannot be overemphasized. Collectors can see the artisans at work in their shops or at craft shows, consider the full range of their offerings in person or through photographs, and, if they wish, even commission pieces to fit special needs or spaces.

When judging modern work, collectors need to add some special questions to their usual list of aesthetic criteria. The best contemporary artisans balance a strong sense of tradition with subtle new approaches of their own. Collectors should therefore ask questions about precedent, innovation, and originality as they consider new baskets. Most important, contem-

porary traditional baskets should fit comfortably within a tradition and demonstrate clear connections to traditional forms, materials, and techniques. Although faithful copies of traditional baskets can please the eye, the mark of truly outstanding work is the way in which the artisan expresses his own personality while still honoring traditional sources.

Great new baskets extend the tradition in some small way, perhaps by experimenting with a new form or decorative technique or by creatively mingling ideas drawn from other traditions. Joyce Schaum, for example, combines elements of traditional Shaker, Native American,

and New England basketry in her own instantly recognizable work, while John McGuire exploits the stylistic range available to the modern craftsperson by making baskets in the three different traditional styles he has mastered: Shaker, Nantucket, and New England.

above: COBRA BASKET WITH HANDLE

Mary Jackson. 1984. Charleston, South Carolina. Bulrush, sweetgrass, longleaf pine needles, palmetto leaf. Private collection. Photograph by Jack Alterman.

below: "Two Lips" Basket
Mary Jackson. 1997. Charleston, South Carolina. Sweetgrass, rush, longleaf pine needles, palmetto. Private collection. Photograph by Jack Alterman. This basket's second lip is formed by the split handle, which is attached to the sides below, and parallel to, the rim. Jackson fashioned the handle from four coils of lighter-colored sweetgrass; pairs of coils are attached on each side of the basket and join together just above the rim.

inch in diameter. The finer coils in turn lent themselves to the creation of smaller, more refined baskets. Sweetgrass baskets, which were sewn with strips of palmetto leaves instead of oak splints, were introduced into the region as early as the 1850s. In contrast to the rush baskets that were made by men and used in the rice fields, sweetgrass baskets were created by women for use in the household, primarily as sewing and yarn baskets.

In 1916 a white Charleston businessman named Clarence Legerton began buying Mount Pleasant sweetgrass baskets to sell in his store and through a mail-order catalog. Legerton's investment in locally made baskets offered a strong new incentive to the Mount Pleasant basketmakers, who eagerly accepted even the small amount of money he paid for their time-consuming work. By the early 1930s, the growth of the local tourist industry and the paving of Route 17, the coastal highway that connects Mount Pleasant and Charleston, offered the area's seagrass basketmakers a chance to control their own business. Setting up stands along the side of the highway, they began selling directly to tourists, thereby cutting out the middlemen and reaping a fuller measure of their work's value. In response to their customers' tastes, they introduced a wide variety of imaginative nonbasket forms aimed at white middle-class women buyers. These included round table mats, hats and hatboxes, bread baskets, trays for cocktail glasses, wastebaskets, and handbags. They also often mixed longleaf pine needles and rush into their coils to produce subtle decorative color accents. The pine needles, which are four to eight inches long, turn dark brown when dry, providing a strong contrast with the light tan of dried sweetgrass. The women worked with the simplest of tools, cutting the ends of the palmetto strips into arrowlike shapes with scissors and then sewing the strips through holes they punched in the grass coils with homemade awls.

Seagrass basketmaking continues to flourish in the Charleston area, where dozens of talented artisans are still active. Seagrass basketmakers are still a common sight along Route 17 as well and

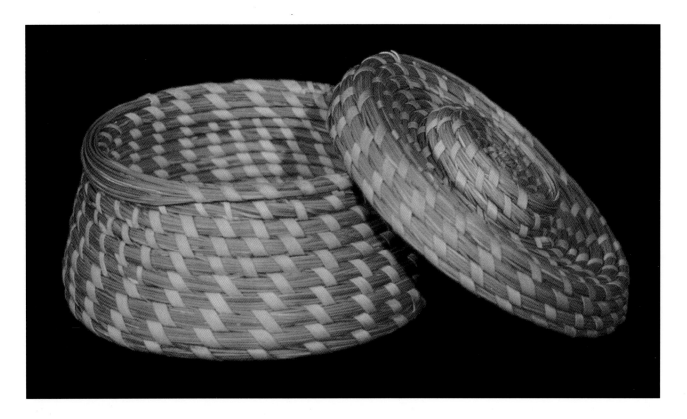

in the markets of downtown Charleston, where they continue to offer their wares to tourists. Although most tourists probably view these baskets primarily as local color, scholars and collectors regard them as works of art. The McKissick Museum at the University of South Carolina in Columbia has been particularly influential in the documentation and preservation of seagrass basketmaking traditions, through their support of groundbreaking research by Dale Rosengarten and by mounting a nationwide exhibition in the late 1980s of old and new baskets, which introduced many people to the art and its history.[25] The McKissick's Folklife Resource Center maintains a varied collection of seagrass baskets and related archival material. Several basketmakers represented in the McKissick exhibition have won national recognition in recent years. Among them is Mary Jane Manigault, who was honored by the National Endowment for the Arts in 1984 as a National Heritage Fellow in recognition of her mastery of traditional arts. Another award-winning artisan is Mary Jackson, an innovative artist whose work is exhibited in a number of important museum collections.

above: COVERED BASKET
Artist unknown. c. 1920. Mount Pleasant, South Carolina. Sweetgrass, palmetto. H: 2¾", D: 5⅛". Charleston Museum, Charleston, South Carolina. Small lidded sweetgrass baskets like this were featured in Charleston entrepreneur Clarence Legerton's mail-order catalog in the 1920s because their simple, compact form was easy to pack and ship.

Today's Mount Pleasant baskets represent a different aesthetic than those of any other American tradition. Their roots lie in Africa, not America or Europe, and their history and development represent a particular part of the African-American experience, articulating a fascinating story of exploitation, pride, regeneration, and cultural survival. Mary Jackson expressed it this way: "My ancestors were far away from their homeland against their will. They were fortunate to have a skill that allowed them to be kept together. The intent of the plantation owners was to separate families so they would lose their identities. Because of the valuable skill [my forebears] had, they could stay together. [They] realized that the baskets would serve as the symbol of why and how they came. They held on to [basketmaking] so that the generations that came would always have and keep their identity with Africa."[26]

Unlike artisans in most other regions of the country, Mount Pleasant basketmakers have also consistently looked beyond basketry for forms and design ideas. Some current basketmakers view their pieces as sculptural works of art that push the boundaries of the utilitarian tradition of the craft. The compressed body and elongated handle of one of Mary Jackson's original designs, for example, do not follow function in the way a fanner basket did. Instead, like a contemporary studio teapot, goblet, or vase, the basket expresses its maker's individual design sensibility in the context of a utilitarian object. It is clearly a basket, and its materials and techniques tie it to a particular tradition, but its form, while still functional, is primarily an aesthetic statement.

As interest in African-American craft and folk art continues to grow, so too does an understanding of its complex sources and its importance in the history of American society and art. Coiled-seagrass basketry is perhaps the oldest surviving African craft still actively practiced in the United States, and its continuing evolution mirrors the identity of the people who have developed it.

above: CAKE BOX BASKET
Mary Habersham. 1979. Mount Pleasant, South Carolina. Sweetgrass, palmetto, pine needles. Museum of International Folk Art, Santa Fe, New Mexico.
The work of an artist who is the third generation of basketmakers in her family.

opposite: BASKET
Mary Jackson. 1997. Charleston, South Carolina. Sweetgrass, rush, longleaf pine needles, palmetto. Private collection. Photograph by Jack Alterman.
Jackson says her goal is to produce "simple yet unique and finely detailed sculpture in which the patterns and symmetry complement each other perfectly."

Collecting and
Caring for Baskets

MERICA'S BASKETS offer the collector a fascinating and
extremely wide range of forms, structures, materials, colors, sizes,
decorative styles, and cultural influences from which to choose.
Baskets exist to suit every taste, temperament, and pocketbook, and
because they are essentially simple, familiar, and unpretentious objects,
they can reward many different levels of appreciation, bringing delight to
both the novice and the scholar. Collectors can consider utilitarian and
decorative baskets, plain and fancy baskets, simple and complex baskets,
woven and coiled baskets, painted and unpainted baskets, ancient and
modern baskets, Native American and African-American baskets. They
might discover a fine old country basket at a garage sale for a few dollars or
pay thousands at auction for a rare and extraordinary example. Aside from
their utilitarian or decorative purposes, baskets connect us to history and
can evoke the spirit of another era or place. As artifacts of our rural, agrarian past, the humble farm baskets of New England or Appalachia, for
example, can help bring the relaxed hominess of country life into even the
most sophisticated city apartment. By contrast, the exotic and intricately
crafted baskets of such Native American tribes as the Pomo or Washo are
often artifacts of the highest artistry, as remarkable and visually striking as
anything ever made in the Americas. Dozens of equally rewarding collecting choices lie between these extremes.

Baskets can fit easily and unobtrusively into virtually any room or
decor. They take up little space and require no special care. Although
some collectors specialize in baskets, most combine them with other
antiques and crafts. Baskets are most often gathered, displayed, and
enjoyed together with related household objects, which help to put them
into historical context and also create a unified decorative scheme. Collectors of Shaker or New England country furniture, for example, often
also collect baskets, which complement their chairs, benches, chests,
desks, and tables, and most collectors of Native American art include baskets among their holdings. Some collectors specialize in baskets from a
particular region or tradition, focusing solely on Nantucket or
Appalachian work, for example, or collecting only baskets made by

below: TWINED BOWL (DETAIL)

Possibly Karok. c. early 1900s. Klamath River, Northern California. Hazel shoots (foundation); conifer roots, bear grass stems, and maidenhair stems (weft). H. 44 cm., D. 40 cm. California Academy of Sciences, San Francisco. Catalog #145-117. Photograph by Dong Lin.

Since they did not make pottery, many California Indian basketmakers crafted tightly woven bowls for preparing or serving food. Karok artisans often decorated their baskets with half-twist overlay, which can be seen only on the outside surface of the basket. In this technique, paired weft strands were worked so the darker colored overlay always faced out.

northwest Indian tribes. Since basket materials and forms have always been intimately related to the plants, landscape, and cultures of the region in which they were made, many collectors concentrate on locally made works. The interior of a spare, weathered old Cape Cod shingled house seems almost incomplete without a few equally chaste lightship baskets on hand, and any well-appointed Appalachian cabin, New England farmhouse, or southwestern adobe home similarly deserves a basket that reflects the history and lifestyles of the region and its people.

Connoisseurship in the study of baskets comes only with time, experience, and a great deal of hard work. As a beginning collector, you should take every opportunity to see outstanding baskets and to compare and contrast the new pieces you encounter. Visit museums, dealers, antique shows, auction houses, and fellow collectors as often as possible. Always look carefully and critically, and always ask questions: Where was this basket made? When? By whom? What materials were used? What methods of

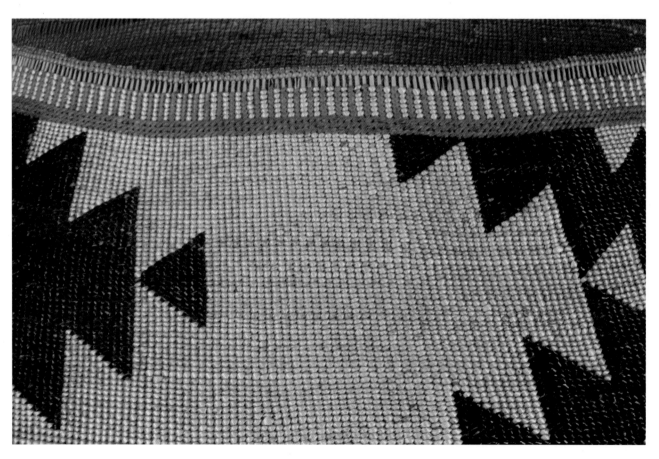

construction and decoration did the artisan use? What was it meant to be used for? Seek out well-informed curators, dealers, and collectors; most experts enjoy sharing their knowledge with someone who is genuinely interested in listening and, especially, in learning.

Contemporary craftspeople who specialize in traditional work can also be immensely helpful. The best of these artisans have done extensive research into the traditions they are helping to keep alive, and their first-hand knowledge of traditional materials and methods can provide much useful information about older baskets. In addition to making and selling their own often superb and highly collectible work, many contemporary craftspeople also teach basketmaking, and even a quick course in the rudiments will add greatly to any collector's understanding and appreciation of what constitutes fine basketry.

The art of basketmaking combines the linear pattern language of weaving with the three-dimensional sculptural forms of pottery, its sister art. It can juxtapose complex structural rhythms and intricate surface detail with fluid and powerful overall form, thus rewarding both intimate examination and long-distance contemplation. When evaluating a basket, the collector therefore needs to consider a number of related factors, including craftsmanship, design, ornamentation, and originality. Three elements should dominate consideration of any basket's aesthetics: the quality of its form and construction, the appeal of any added paint or decoration, and the condition of the basket. First, consider its proportions. Look at it from a distance to isolate its sculptural shape. The various structural elements of the basket should work together to create a pleasing overall form. The handle or handles, if present, should flow harmoniously out of the basket's body, and the weave structure should complement the basket's size and shape. Be aware that baskets are tactile objects, meant to be touched and held. Consider how the basket feels; savor its heft and balance, the tight smoothness of its construction, the contrast between its lightness and its structural strength, the way its handle fits into your hand or its base nestles into your lap.

Judge whether the basketmaker was a master of the medium and whether the methods and materials he or she used are appropriate to this particular basket. Look for fine details of craftsmanship; tightly sewn coiling, an unusually complex weave, an especially imaginative or innovative use of materials, or a particularly well-shaped handle, for example, can increase a basket's value significantly. So can a rare form. Oval Nantucket baskets are far less common than round examples, for instance, and a nest of ovals can bring a premium. Particularly large or small examples of a particular form are often more valuable than ordinary sizes, and an uncommon handle form or a construction variation may also increase the value of a piece.

Condition is a major factor in value. Damage and repaired spots are most often found at stress points—on the lid, on the bottom, or along ribs and seams. Examine baskets carefully, turning them over and looking at all sides of both the outside and inside surfaces. Some signs of wear on utilitarian baskets are perfectly acceptable, even desirable, as long as they do not detract from the overall appearance of the piece. In contrast, baskets that were originally intended for decorative or ceremonial purposes should be as pristine as possible. Be sure the materials are consistent. Since many baskets saw hard everyday use, old repairs may be acceptable if they are unobtrusive and not extensive and if they were carefully done. If you are in doubt about whether a basket has been repaired, however, the best course is often to walk away and find a different one.

Like any antique, an old basket should have a warm, mellow patina of age, its surface pleasingly darkened and mottled by the combined effects of oxidation, accumulated dirt, and use. While patina can be faked, few deceivers take the time to re-create the varied and uneven results of many years of wear. Watch out for uniformly darkened surfaces or artificial aging, which wily sellers may achieve quickly by treating baskets with oils or dipping them in "teas." Painted surfaces should also show their age. Colors should be softened and muted by time, although any designs on the surface of a basket should still be clearly defined. Collectors of painted baskets should study typical examples in order to identify unusual colors and patterns that will add interest and value because of their rarity.

Handle old baskets gently. Handles and rims are particularly vulnerable and should be treated with respect; never pick an unfamiliar old basket up by its handle. Baskets should be dusted occasionally with a soft brush (paintbrushes work well), feather duster, or dry cloth. When dusting, be aware of any mildew, cracking of fibers or paints, changes in color, or damage by insects or rodents who eat plant fiber. A few mothballs placed near—but not directly touching—your baskets can offer some protection. Wrap the repellent in plastic or some other impregnable material if you must place it inside the basket. Do not bathe or soak your baskets in water. Patina—the accumulated evidence of age and wear—is a critical component of an antique basket's identity and can all too easily be scrubbed away by an uninformed owner. If an unpainted basket is caked with dirt when you acquire it, you may be able to sponge it gently with distilled water without risking damage. Water can leave permanent spots on splint baskets, however, so it's a good idea to test the bottom first. If any part of the basket's surface is painted or dyed, be sure to test a small, inconspicuous spot before you proceed; many vegetable dyes are volatile and easily damaged. If you have any doubt, consult a professional conservator. Most major natural history and art museums have conservators on staff, and their expertise can be invaluable—indeed priceless.

Nothing other than water or specially formulated solvents should ever be applied to a basket's surface. Shellac and varnish, which creates a horribly glossy and completely uniform surface, are anathema to serious collectors and will completely destroy the value of any basket. Also avoid the common mistake of oiling your baskets. Linseed oil is particularly insidious; it will imitate the effects of age by darkening and adding a pleasing sheen to a basket in the short term, but over time it will attract and retain dirt until the surface is black. Unfortunately, the effects of linseed oil are

above: FIBONACCI 21

Billy Ruth Suddoth. 1998. Bakersville, North Carolina. European reed splint dyed with walnut hulls and iron oxide. 15" x 17" x 17". Private collection.

Fibonacci (c. 1170–1250) was an Italian mathematician who developed "The Nature Sequence," a series of ratios found in the spacing of spiral growth in such natural objects as seashells and flowers. Suddoth says, "I use the Fibonacci numbers in my baskets. The rhythm of the pattern seems predetermined as if by nature itself. [My baskets] are both visual and tactile, inviting the viewer to touch and explore with the eyes and hands. I do not separate myself from nature, but through my weaving affirm being part of it."

cumulative and largely irreversible. The strands of its molecules cross-link chemically with accumulated dirt within the pores of the wood, congealing and eventually forming an impenetrable layer of sludge that will completely mask a basket's original color and decoration.

You should also be careful not to expose your baskets to direct sunlight, which will bleach and crack painted or dyed surfaces. Additionally, sunlight degrades straw, grasses, and other plant fibers very quickly. Fluorescent lights also produce damaging ultraviolet rays, so you should fit them with UV filters (available from museum supply houses) or place the basket elsewhere. Because dry baskets can become brittle and fragile, keep the humidity level in your home as constant as possible. Be aware that while wood expands as it absorbs moisture and contracts as it dries, painted surfaces do not. You can therefore help prevent cracking and damaging paint by avoiding extreme swings in humidity. Collectors who live in highly variable northern climates, where winter heating can create near desert conditions, should have a humidifier running during the dry months.

Collectors can display their treasures in many different ways. Some like to group a few baskets on tables, chests, or work counters, similar to the way our ancestors probably stored them. Other people stack their baskets together in cupboards or on mantelpieces or arrange them in corners and other less-trafficked parts of the house. Because baskets come in so many variations, they offer endless possibilities to creative designers and decorators. Their contrasting sizes, colors, patterns, textures, and forms offer myriad ways to create pleasing visual rhythms. Covered baskets such as those made by woodland Indians can be stacked atop one another to great effect, for example, and flat baskets such as Nez Percé bags, Hopi trays, seagrass fanners, and openwork cheese baskets look elegant hanging against an otherwise bare wall. Baskets with sturdy, well-attached handles can be hung from hooks, pegs, overhead racks, exposed beams, or hat trees. Baskets can also lend themselves to a more formal, museumlike setting, if you wish to create a showy and protective environment for prized examples. Some collectors house outstanding examples in glass cases in their living room or den. Others draw attention to special baskets by mounting them on freestanding wooden platforms of different heights. These platforms can be covered with protective Plexiglas hoods and lit by track spotlights, but such a formal presentation is unnecessary to enjoy a basket's beauty. Local museums can usually provide advice on building or purchasing special exhibit cases and lighting.

The finest baskets are unquestionably works of art, and owners should, of course, appreciate them for their fine craftsmanship and creative design. But the serious collector should always be aware that they were crafted foremost as useful objects, made for a specific reason within a specific human community. Craftsmanship and use, along with form and function, are inextricably intertwined in traditional basketry, and the value of a utilitarian or ceremonial basket is diminished if a collector does not appreciate them both. The more you know about the cultural context within which a basket was made and used, the more you can appreciate its particular meaning and significance and the intentions of its maker.

These connections are, unfortunately, often difficult to discover. Since most baskets were inexpensive practical objects, their original owners largely discounted their artistic merit and relatively few contemporary records about them exist. Baskets were rarely included in household estate inventories, for example, and contemporary observers wrote little about the basketmakers or their work. Similarly, today's collectors and dealers rarely have time to do more than pass on whatever scraps of information they might know or guess about a basket. Even in museum collections, few baskets are well documented, and until recently, only Native American works received serious attention from scholars and researchers. Collectors should therefore cherish every bit of information they can gather about the history of a particular basket, and they should appreciate the importance of preserving precious data.

While baskets were made for everyday use, these humble utilitarian objects often reveal an artistry and integrity that has outlasted and transcended their original functions. Their forms, materials, techniques, and decorations all reflect the personal and cultural identity of their makers and often embody the spirit of the ethnic and regional traditions in which they were made and used. It is therefore the task of today's collector to attempt to reconnect historic baskets with their traditions and link aesthetic, functional, and cultural appreciation into a unified understanding. With such a union, historians, artisans, museums, collectors, and anyone else involved with the ancient craft will know how these deceptively simple objects have carried significant meaning across time and between peoples.

following page: PRESIDENTIAL FISHING CREEL
Daryl and Karen Arawjo. 1992. Bushkill, Pennsylvania. Handsplit white oak, cherry lid with inlay. 9" x 7" x 14". Private collection.

Selected Resources

ANTIQUE DEALERS AND
AUCTION HOUSES

Butterfield and Butterfield
220 San Bruno Avenue
San Francisco, CA 94103
*Native American art auctions often
include baskets*

Christie's
502 Park Avenue
New York, NY 10022
*Native American art auctions often
include baskets*

Suzanne Courcier and Robert
Wilkins
Route 22
Austerlitz, NY 12017
*Shaker antiques and folk art including
baskets*

Larry Hackley/Bluegrassroots
Box 88
North Middleton, KY 40357
*Folk art from Kentucky and the South
including regional baskets*

Willis Henry Auctions
22 Main Street
Marshfield, MA 02050
Shaker antiques including baskets

Paul Madden Antiques
146 Main Street
Sandwich, MA 02563
Nantucket baskets

Morning Star Gallery
513 Canyon Road
Santa Fe, NM 87501
Southwestern Indian baskets

Rafael Osona
21 Washington Street
Nantucket, MA 02554
*Nantucket auctions often include
baskets*

Wayne Pratt and Company
28 Main Street
Nantucket, MA 02554
*American antiques including Nantucket
baskets*

Richard and Betty Ann Rasso
Village Square
East Chatham, NY 12060
*American folk art and accessories
including Shaker, New England, and
Eastern Indian baskets*

David A. Schorsch American
Antiques, Inc.
44 Main Street South
Woodbury, CT 06798
*American folk art including New En-
gland, Shaker, and Eastern Indian
baskets*

Skinner, Inc.
Route 117
Bolton, MA 01740
*Native American art and Shaker auc-
tions often include baskets*

Sotheby's
1334 York Avenue
New York, NY 10021
*Native American art auctions often
include baskets*

MUSEUMS

**African-American Seagrass
Baskets**

Atlanta Historical Society
3101 Andrews Drive, N.W.
Atlanta, GA 30305

Charleston Museum
360 Meeting Street
Charleston, SC 29403

McKissick Museum
University of South Carolina
Pendleton and Bull Streets
Columbia, SC 29208

Y. W. Bailey Museum
Box 126
Lands End Road
Saint Helena, SC 29220

American Indian Baskets

Abbe Museum
Box 286
Bar Harbor, ME 04609
Baskets by Maine tribes

American Indian Archaeological
Institute
Box 1260
Washington Green, CT 06783-
0260
Northeastern tribes

California Academy of the Sciences
Golden Gate Park
San Francisco, CA 94118
Aleut, California, and Southwest tribes

Fenimore House Museum
Thaw Collection of Native Ameri-
can Art
Box 800
Cooperstown, NY 11326
Baskets from several different regions

Field Museum
Roosevelt Road at Lake Shore
Drive
Chicago, IL 60605
All regions

Haffenreffer Museum of
Anthropology
Brown University
Bristol, RI 02809
All regions

Heard Museum
22 East Monte Vista Road
Phoenix, AZ 85004
Southwestern focus

Hood Museum of Art
Dartmouth College
Hanover, NH 03755
All regions

Lauren Rogers Museum of Art
Box 1108
Laurel, MS 39441
All regions

Maine State Museum
State House Station 83
Augusta, ME 04333
Baskets by Maine tribes

Maine Tribal Unity Museum
Quaker Hill Road
Unity, ME 04988
Over 500 baskets by Maine tribes

Museum of International Folk Art
Box 2087
Santa Fe, NM 87504-2087
All regions; includes contemporary work

Museum of the Cherokee Indian
Box 1599
Cherokee, NC 28719

National Museum of the American
Indian, Smithsonian Institution
George Gustave Heye Center
One Bowling Green
New York, NY 10004
All regions

Natural History Museum of Los
Angeles County
900 Exposition Boulevard
Los Angeles, CA 90007
California tribes

Peabody Essex Museum
East India Square
Salem, MA 01970
All regions

Peabody Museum of Archaeology
and Ethnology
Harvard University
11 Divinity Avenue
Cambridge, MA 02138
All regions. Includes important early baskets collected by first-contact explorers like Meriwether Lewis.

Philbrook Museum of Art
Box 52510
Tulsa, OK 74152
Southwest and Great Basin

San Diego Museum of Man
1350 El Prado
Balboa Park
San Diego, CA 92101
All regions

School of American Research
Box 2188
Santa Fe, NM 87504
Southwestern focus

Southwest Museum
Box 41558
Los Angeles, CA 90041-0558
Western focus

Appalachian Baskets

Appalachian Museum
Berea College
Berea, KY 40404

Blue Ridge Institute
Ferrum College
Ferrum, VA 24088

Museum of Appalachia
Box 359, Highway 61
Norris, TN 37826

Nantucket Baskets

Heritage Plantation of Sandwich
Box 566
Sandwich, MA 02563

Nantucket Historical Association
Box 1016
Nantucket, MA 02554

New England Baskets

Farmer's Museum
New York State Historical
Association
Box 800
Cooperstown, NY 13326

Maine State Museum
State House Station 83
Augusta, ME 04333

Old Sturbridge Village
Sturbridge, MA 01566

Shelburne Museum
Box 10
Shelburne, VT 05482

Society for the Preservation of
New England Antiquities
141 Cambridge Street
Boston, MA 02114

Pennsylvania German Baskets

Landis Valley Museum/Pennsylvania Farm Museum
2451 Kissel Hill Road
Lancaster, PA 17601

Mercer Museum
84 South Pine Street
Doylestown, PA 18901

Shaker Baskets

Shaker Village, Inc.
Box 288
Canterbury, NH 03224

Fruitlands Museums
102 Prospect Hill
Harvard, MA 01451

Hancock Shaker Village, Inc.
Box 898
Pittsfield, MA 01202

Shaker Museum
Old Chatham, NY 12136

Shaker Museum at South Union
South Union, KY 42283

Shaker Village of Pleasant Hill
3500 Lexington Road
Harrodsburg, KY 40330

United Society of Shakers, Sabbathday Lake
RR 1, Box 640
Poland Spring, ME 04274

TRADITIONAL BASKET ARTISANS AND ORGANIZATIONS

Daryl and Karen Arawjo
Box 477
Bushkill, PA 18324-0477
White oak baskets in many styles

California Indian Basketmakers
Association
16894 China Flats Road
Nevada City, CA 95959
Over 200 Native American artisans

Thelma Davis Hibdon
Route 2, Box 167
Woodbury, TN 37190
Appalachian white oak basketry

Indian Arts and Crafts Board
Room 4004N
U.S. Dept. of the Interior
Washington, DC 20240

Gerrie Kennedy
Box 85
Worthington, MA 02540
Shaker fancy baskets

Jonathan Kline
5066 Mott Evans Road
Trumansburg, NY 14886
Black ash basketry

Maine Indian Basketmakers
Alliance
c/o Penobscot Indian Nation
6 River Road
Indian Island, ME 04468

Tom and Connie McColley
Route 3, Box 325
Chloe, WV 25235
Nontraditional white oak basketry

John McGuire
398 South Main Street
Geneva, NY 14456
New England, Shaker, and Nantucket baskets

Mount Pleasant Sweetgrass Basket-
makers Association
Box 761
Mount Pleasant, SC 29424

North Carolina Basketmakers
Association
5117 Carter Street
Raleigh, NC 27612
Annual March convention includes artists and teachers from all over the country.

Northwest Indian Basketweavers
Association
Coleen Ray, Director
6835 Zangle Road
Olympia, WA 98506

Susi Nuss
5 Steele Crossing Road
Bolton, CT 06043
Black ash basketry

Joyce Schaum
2212 Reifsnider Road
Keymar, MD 21757
Ash and reed basketry, influenced by Shaker and Native American patterns

Southern Highland Handicraft
Guild
Box 9545
Asheville, NC 28815
Appalachian white oak and other regional styles and materials by many different artisans

Southwestern Association for
Indian Arts, Inc.
Box 31066
Santa Fe, NM 87594-1066
Maintains a database of approximately 1600 Native American artisans work-ing in a variety of media. "The Art of Basketmaking," a buyer's guide to southwestern Indian basketry, available.

Marie Elena Stotler
23 Frame Avenue
Malvern, PA 19355
Rye straw, especially skeps

Cynthia W. Taylor and Aaron Yakim
2605 Cypress Street
Parkersburg, WV 26101
Appalachian white oak basketry

Karen and Chris Waldron
Lick Log Mill Store
4321 Dillard Road, SR 106
Highland, NC 28741
704-526-3934

Martha Wetherbee Basket Shop
HCR 69, Box 116
Sanbornton, NH 03269
Shaker baskets, kits, and classes

Stephen Zeh
Box 381
Temple, ME 04984
Maine brown ash

Notes

1. Ed Rossbach, *The Nature of Basketry* (West Chester, Pennsylvania: Schiffer Publications, 1986), p. 187.

2. Edward Lucie-Smith, *The Story of Craft: The Craftsman's Role in Society* (Ithaca, New York: Cornell University Press, 1981), pp. 24–25.

3. Sarah H. Hill, *Weaving New Worlds: Southeastern Cherokee Women and Their Basketry* (Chapel Hill: University of North Carolina Press, 1997), p. 325.

4. Tom Hill and Richard W. Hill Sr., eds., *Creation's Journey: Native American Identity and Belief* (Washington: Smithsonian Institution Press, 1997), p. 117.

5. For a fascinating analysis of the meaning of gift-giving in northwest coast societies, see Lewis Hyde, *The Gift: Imagination and the Erotic Life of Property* (New York: Vintage Books, 1979).

6. George Wharton James, *Indian Basketry* (1909; reprint, New York: Dover Publications, 1972), pp. 115–16.

7. James, op. cit., p. 224.

8. Quoted in the *California Indian Basketweavers Association Newsletter*, June 1997.

9. "Helping to Weave the Dream," *American Craft*, April–May 1995, p. 9.

10. Quoted in the *California Indian Basketweavers Association Newsletter*, June 1997.

11. Quoted in Peter J. Stephano, "Split-Ash Baskets Maine Style," *Wood Magazine*, September 1992.

12. Jane Beck, ed., *Always in Season* (Montpelier: Vermont Historical Society, 1981).

13. See Martha Wetherbee and Nathan Taylor, *Shaker Baskets* (Sanbornton, New Hampshire: Martha Wetherbee Basket Shop, 1988), p. 164.

14. Quoted in David H. Wood, *The Lightship Baskets of Nantucket: A Continuing Craft.* (Nantucket, Massachusetts: Nantucket Historical Association, 1994), p. 8.

15. Wood is currently at work on a book that will document his findings, gathered over dozens of years of research on the island.

16. Beatrice Garvan and Charles F. Hummel, *The Pennsylvania Germans: A Celebration of Their Arts* (Philadelphia: Philadelphia Museum of Art, 1975), p. 8.

17. Marie Elena Stotler, letter to the author, February 1998.

18. The term was popularized by John C. Campbell in his book, *The Southern Highlander and His Homeland* (New York: Russell Sage Foundation, 1921).

19. David Hackett Fischer. *Albion's Seed: Four British Folkways in America* (New York: Oxford University Press, 1989), pp. 605–782.

20. Allen H. Eaton. *Handicrafts of the Southwestern Highlands* (New York: Russell Sage Foundation, 1937), p. 44.

21. Ibid., p. 31.

22. Ibid., p. 174.

23. From a biography supplied by Yakim and Taylor.

24. Personal correspondence with author, October 30, 1991.

25. Dale Rosengarten. *Row upon Row: Sea Grass Baskets of the South Carolina Lowlands* (Columbia: McKissick Museum, University of South Carolina, 1986).

26. Barbara Glass, ed. *Uncommon Beauty in Common Objects: The Legacy of African-American Craft Art* (Wilberforce, Ohio: National Afro-American Museum and Cultural Center, 1993), p. 19.

For Further Reading

Andrews, Edward Deming. *The Community Industries of the Shakers.* Albany: University of the State of New York, 1932.

———. *The People Called Shakers: A Search for the Perfect Society.* New York: Dover Publications, 1953.

———, and Faith Andrews. *Work and Worship among the Shakers.* New York: Dover Publications, 1974.

Ballantine, Betty, and Ian Ballantine. *The Native Americans: An Illustrated History.* Atlanta: Turner Publishing, 1993.

Bibby, Brian. *The Fine Art of California Indian Basketry.* Sacramento: Crocker Art Museum with Heyday Books, 1996.

Billard, Jules B., ed. *The World of the American Indian.* Washington: National Geographic Society, 1974.

Curtis, Edward Sheriff. *The North American Indian.* New York: Taschen America, 1997.

Eaton, Allen. *Handicrafts of New England.* New York: Harper, 1949.

———. *Handicrafts of the Southern Highlands.* New York: Russell Sage Foundation, 1937; reprint, New York: Dover Publications, 1973.

Eckstorm, Fannie Hardy. *Bulletin III: The Handicrafts of the Modern Indians of Maine,* 1932; reprint, Bar Harbor, Maine: Robert Abbe Museum, 1980.

Fane, Diana, Ira Jacknis, and Lise M. Breen. *Objects of Myth and Memory: American Indian Art at the Brooklyn Museum.* Brooklyn: Brooklyn Museum with University of Washington Press, 1991.

Fischer, David Hackett. *Albion's Seed: Four British Folkways in America.* New York: Oxford University Press, 1989.

Furst, Peter T., and Jill L. Furst. *North American Indian Art.* New York: Rizzoli, 1982.

Garvan, Beatrice B. *The Pennsylvania German Collection.* Philadelphia: Philadelphia Museum of Art, 1982.

Handsman, Russell G., and Ann McMullen, eds. *A Key into the Language of Woodsplint Baskets.* Washington, Connecticut: American Indian Archaeological Institute, 1987.

Hedges, Ken. *Fibers and Forms: Native American Basketry of the West.* San Diego: San Diego Museum of Man, 1997.

Hill, Sarah H. *Weaving New Worlds: Southeastern Cherokee Women and Their Basketry.* Chapel Hill: University of North Carolina Press, 1997.

Hill, Tom, and Richard W. Hill Sr., eds. *Creation's Journey: Native American Identity and Belief.* Washington: Smithsonian Institution Press, 1997.

Houlihan, Patrick, Jerold L. Collings, Sarah Nestor, and Jonathan Batkin. *Harmony by Hand: Art of the Southwest Indians.* San Francisco: Chronicle Books, 1987.

Hyde, Lewis. *The Gift: Imagination and the Erotic Life of Property.* New York: Vintage Books, 1979.

Irwin, John Rice. *Baskets and Basket Makers in Southern Appalachia.* West Chester, Pennsylvania: Schiffer Publications, 1982.

James, George Wharton. *Indian Basketry.* 1909. Reprint, New York: Dover Publications, 1972.

Josephy, Alvin M., Jr. *The Indian Heritage of America.* Boston: Houghton Mifflin, 1968. Reprint, 1991.

Joyce, Rosemary O. *A Bearer of Tradition: Dwight Stump, Basketmaker.* Athens: University of Georgia Press, 1989.

Kardon, Janet, ed. *Revivals! Diverse Traditions.* New York: Harry N. Abrams, with the American Craft Museum, 1994.

Kennedy, Gerrie, Galen Beale, and Jim Johnson. *Shaker Baskets and Poplarware: A Field Guide.* Vol. 3. Stockbridge, Massachusetts: Berkshire House, 1992.

Ketchum, William C., Jr. *American Basketry and Woodenware.* New York: Macmillan, 1974.

Lampell, Ramona, and Millard Lampell, with David Larkin. *O Appalachia: Artists of the Southern Mountains.* New York: Stewart, Tabori and Chang, 1989.

Lasansky, Jeannette. *Willow, Oak and Rye: Basket Traditions in Pennsylvania.* University Park: Pennsylvania State University Press, 1979.

Law, Rachel Nash, and Cynthia Taylor. *Appalachian White Oak Basketmaking: Handing Down the Tradition.* Knoxville: University of Tennessee Press, 1991.

Lobb. Allan. *Indian Baskets of the Pacific Northwest and Alaska.* Portland, Oregon: Graphic Arts Center, 1990.

Lucie-Smith, Edward. *The Story of Craft: The Craftsman's Role in Society.* Ithaca, New York: Cornell University Press, 1981.

Mason, Otis Tufton. "Aboriginal American Basketry: Studies in a Textile Art without Machinery." *Annual Report of the*

Smithsonian Institution. Washington: Government Printing Office, 1904.

Mauldin, Barbara. *Traditions in Transition: Contemporary Basket Weaving of the Southwestern Indians.* Santa Fe: Museum of New Mexico Press, 1949.

Maxwell, James A. *America's Fascinating Indian Heritage.* Pleasantville, New York: Reader's Digest Association, 1978.

McGuire, John. *Basketry—The Shaker Tradition.* Asheville, North Carolina: Lark Books, 1988.

Penney, David. *Native American Art.* Southport, Connecticut: Hugh Lauter Levin Associates, 1994.

Pulleyn, Rob, ed. *The Basketmaker's Art: Contemporary Baskets and Their Makers.* Asheville, North Carolina: Lark Books, 1986.

Rosengarten, Dale. *Row upon Row: Sea Grass Baskets of the South Carolina Lowlands.* Columbia: McKissick Museum, University of South Carolina, 1986.

Rossbach, Ed. *Baskets as Textile Art.* West Chester, Pennsylvania: Schiffer Publications, 1986.

Schorsch, David A. *American Baskets: A Folk Art Tradition.* New York: David A. Schorsch, 1988.

Shaw, Robert. *America's Traditional Crafts.* Southport, Connecticut: Hugh Lauter Levin Associates, 1993.

Siporin, Steve. *American Masters: The National Heritage Fellows.* New York: Harry N. Abrams with the Museum of International Folk Art, Santa Fe, 1992.

Sprigg, June. *By Shaker Hands.* New York: Knopf, 1975.

———. *Shaker Design.* New York: Whitney Museum with Norton, 1986.

———, and David Larkin. *Shaker: Life, Work and Art.* New York: Stewart, Tabori and Chang, 1987.

Tanner, Clara Lee. *Apache Indian Baskets.* Tucson: University of Arizona, 1982.

———. *Indian Baskets of the Southwest.* Tucson: University of Arizona, 1983.

Teleki, Gloria Roth. *The Baskets of Rural America.* New York: Dutton, 1975.

———. *Collecting Traditional American Basketry.* New York: Dutton, 1979.

Turnbaugh, Sarah Peabody, and William A. Turnbaugh.

Indian Baskets. West Chester, Pennsylvania: Schiffer Publications, 1986.

Vlach, John Michael. *The Afro-American Tradition in Decorative Arts.* Cleveland: Cleveland Museum of Art, 1978.

Waters, Frank. *The Book of the Hopi.* New York: Penguin, 1972.

Wetherbee, Martha, and Nathan Taylor. *Shaker Baskets.* Sanbornton, New Hampshire: Martha Wetherbee Basket Shop, 1988.

Whiteford, Andrew Hunter. *Southwestern Indian Baskets: Their History and Their Makers.* Santa Fe: School of American Research Press, 1988.

———, and Kate McGraw. *The Art of Basketmaking: A Buyer's Guide to Southwestern Indian Basketry.* Santa Fe: Southwestern Association for Indian Arts, 1994.

Wood, David H. *The Lightship Baskets of Nantucket: A Continuing Craft.* Nantucket, Massachusetts: Nantucket Historical Association, 1994.

———. "Nantucket Lightship Baskets: Origins and Variations." *The Magazine Antiques,* August 1995.

Yanagai, Soetsu. Adapted and introduced by Bernard Leach. *The Unknown Craftsman: A Japanese Insight into Beauty.* New York and Tokyo: Kodansha International, 1972.

Glossary

ANILINE DYE: A type of brightly colored chemical dye derived from coal tar and first employed by Indian basketmakers in the 1870s.

BAIL: Overhead handle, usually movable.

BALEEN: Keratinous material found in the mouths of nontoothed whales and used to strain krill shrimp from ingested seawater.

BUTTOCKS BASKET: Round-bottomed ribbed form common in Appalachia and named for its resemblance to human buttocks.

CATHEAD: A Shaker basket form named for the unusual profile of its bottom.

CHAFF: Husks of grain.

COILED: Basket made by sewing bundles of grass or similar material together in circular forms.

COOPER: A tradesperson who crafts wooden barrels.

DOUBLE-WOVEN: A two-layered basket with one layer woven to fit tightly inside the other.

FALSE EMBROIDERY: A decorative technique employed in some twined baskets, created by wrapping single strands of colored material around the outside edge of the weft strands while weaving, and therefore seen only on the outside of the basket.

FANCY BASKETS: A decorative basket intended more for show than for use.

FRIENDSHIP BASKET: A form of covered purse basket invented and popularized by Nantucket artisan José Formoso Reyes. The Taconic artisan Frank Hotaling also dubbed one of his gift basket forms "friendship baskets."

GAUGE: A tool used to cut basket splint into strips of equal width.

KITTENHEAD: A miniature cathead basket.

KRILL: Tiny saltwater shrimp; favored food of nontoothed whales.

MOLD: A wooden form over which a basket is shaped.

PLAITED: Basket made by weaving pieces of splint at right angles to each other.

PORCUPINE WORK: Decorative twists or curls of weft splint that stick out from the plaited weave to create a three-dimensional surface.

RATTAN: The favored material of Nantucket basketmakers, produced from the stems of a climbing tropical palm.

RYESTRAW: A tall grain native to Europe; its strands were the favored material of German immigrant basketmakers in the United States.

SEAGRASS: Any coastal grass used as a basketmaking material. The best-known seagrass baskets are those of African-American basketmakers of the Southeast. Also called sweetgrass.

SKEP: A dome-shaped beehive often made from coiled ryestraw.

SPLINT: Thin, flat strips of hardwood used for plaiting.

SPLIT: A strip of woodsplint.

STUFF: Traditional basketmakers' term for basketmaking material.

SWING HANDLE: A movable overhead handle.

TWILLED: A plaited basket in which warp and weft pass over and under each other at intervals greater than the width of one row.

TWINED: A basket made by weaving two or more weft elements between warp elements. Both warp and weft are usually pliable.

WARP: The vertical elements in a woven structure.

WEFT: The horizontal elements in a woven structure.

WINNOW: To separate hulled kernels of grain from their husks, or chaff.

Index

Italic page numbers indicate illustration captions.

African-Americans, 17, *21*, 187–98, 199
Aleuts, 17, 31–36
Algonquin Indians, 87–88
Anasazi culture, 68, 69–70
Appalachia, 17, 25
    Cherokee baskets, 83, 84–85
    crafts revival, 175, 178
    immigrant baskets, 163–186, 199
    Shaker baskets, 128, *131*
Arrowmont, 175
ash trees, 110–11

Basketmakers, 69–70
beehive basket, *155*, 159–60
Benson, Mary, 62
Berea College, 175
black ash, 85, 92, 110–11, 113, 124, 140
Boler, Daniel, *119*, *120*, 128
Boyer, Sherman, 153
bread-raising basket, 159, *161*
bulrush, 188, 191
Burton, A. O., 185

California and Great Basin Indians, 17, 21, 24, 49–66, *202*
California Indian Basketweavers Association, 64, 65
Campbell, Ben Nighthorse, 65
cathead forms, 128, 132
cattails, 70
cedar bark strips, 38, 39
ceremonial baskets, 23–24, 52–53, 70
Charleston, S.C., 194–95
Cherokee Indians, 77, 79, 80, 83–85
Chesney, Ralph, *175*, 185
Chinook Indians, 38
Chitimacha Indians, 17, 77, 79, 80, 84
Choctaw Indians, 80
Chumash Indians, 53
Cohn, Abram, 56, 62
coiled baskets, 20, 21
    African-American seagrass, *21*, *187*, 188, 191, 192, 194, 197
    California Indians, 51, 59, *61*
    German-Americans, 159
    Great Basin Indians, 53, 55, 56
    Southwest Indians, 69, 70, 71, 72, 75
collecting, 61, 94, 153, 185, 193, 199–205
    caring for baskets, 202–4
    displaying baskets, 204–5
    evaluating baskets, 201–202
Columbia County, N.Y., 136

Cook, James, 39, 41
Cook, Lucy and William Cody, 185

Datsolalee, 56, *61*, 62
Davis, Denise, *64*, *65*
Davis, Ida Pearl, 178, 185
decorated baskets
    California Indians, *202*
    Nantucket, 151
    Northeast Indians, 92–93, 94, 95–96
    Pacific Northwest Indians, 33–34, 38–39
    Southeast Indians, 84
    Southwest Indians, 71, 75
decoy baskets, 55
degikups, 56, *61*, 62
Desert Culture, 15–16
devil's-claw, 55, *67*, 72, 75
Dolly basket, *163*
Dominguez, Dee, 64–65
double-weave twill, 84
duck decoys, 55
dyes, 39, 45, 71, 80, 84, 85, 93, 94, 178
Dysart, Lena and Flora, 185

Eaton, Allen, 164, 167, 185
Eye, Levi, 167

fancy baskets, Shaker, 128–29, 132, 141
feather baskets, 106–7
feathered baskets, 52–53, *61*, 62
fishermen's baskets, 107, 109, *205*
flat-twined wallets, 45
Folger, George, 153
friendship baskets
    Nantucket, *150*, 151
    Taconic, *140*, 141

galleta grass, 71
gathering baskets, 45, *62*
German immigrants, 17, 136–37, 155–62
gift baskets, 52–53
Graham, Alfred, 192
grass baskets, 70
Great Basin Indians, 17, 21, 53–66
Greensfelder, Sara, 65
Gullah culture, 17, 192

Haida Indians, 38, 39
Hall, Davis, 146, 150, *151*, 153
Hancock Shaker Village, Mass., 131, 132, 137
Harris, Henry ("Hen Pen"), 94
hats, basket, *37*, 39–41
Havasupai Indians, *68*, 70
Herger, Wally, 65

Hibdon, Thelma, 178
hickory splint, 137
Hickox, Elizabeth Conrad, 62
Hill, Sarah H., 25, 27
Hohokam culture, 68
honeysuckle baskets, 85, *171*
Hopi Indians, 23, *67*, 69, 70, 71–72, *75*
Hotaling, Frank, *140*
Hupa Indians, *49*, 53
Hussey, Christopher, 144

immigrant traditions, 1, 99–206

Jackson, Andrew, 83
Jackson, Mary, *27*, *187*, *194*, 195, 197
James, George Wharton, 56, 61
Jones, Dan and Martha, 185
Jones, Jessie, 185
Joyce, Rosemary O., 25

kachinas, 71
Karok Indians, *49*, 53, *200*
Kennedy, Gerrie, *119*, 132
Keyser, Louisa, 56, 61, 62
kittenhead forms, 129, 132
Klamath Indians, 53
Kline, Jonathan, *101*, 116, 141, 193
Kwakiutl Indians, 38, 39

Lasansky, Jeannette, 25
Law, Rachel Nash, 25, 181
Lee, Ann, 120, 121, 132
Legerton, Clarence, 194
Lewis, Meriwether, 39, 41
lightship baskets, 17, *145*, 146, 150, 153
Little, Nina and Bertram, 153
Lyon, Carrie, 185

Maidu Indians, 53, *62*, *64*
Malone, Jennifer, *64*
Manigault, Mary Jane, *191*, 195
Marshall, John, 83
Mason, Otis Tufton, 61
McCarter, Mac, 185
McColley, Connie and Tom, 181
McGuire, John, 141, 193
McKissick Museum, 195
measuring baskets, 109
Micmac Indians, 89
miniature baskets, *137*, 140, 153, *171*
Mohegan Indians, 89, *94*
Mohegan pink, 93
molds, 95, *124*, 125, *128*, 145, 146
Mono Indians, 54, *64*
Mount Lebanon, N.Y., 128, 137

Mount Pleasant, S.C., *21*, 25, 192–97
museums, 55, 131, 195

Nantucket Island, 17, 142–154
Natchez Indians, 78
National Endowment for the Arts, 65, 80, 195
National Heritage Fellow, 80, 195
Native American traditions, 15–17, 20, 21,
    23–24, 25, 27, 29–98, 199, *202*
    as immigrant influence, 109–10, 116
Navajo Indians, 70
nested baskets, *78, 135*, 146, *151*, 153
Newell, Eddie, 116
New England, 17
    immigrant baskets, 101–18, 199
    Indian baskets, *16*, 87–93
    Nantucket baskets, 142–54
    Shaker-influenced baskets, 132
New South Shoal (lightship), 146, 150, *151*
New York, 87, 94, 120, 136–44
Nicholson, Grace, 62
Nicholson, Oral, 179
Nicholson, Silas, 185
Nootka Indians, 38
North Carolina, 83, 84, 175
Northeast Indians, 87–98
Nuss, Susi, 193

oak rod baskets, 172
oak splint, 84, 137, 140, 171
Old Town, Maine, 94
ollas (storage jars), 75
Owsley, Bird, 185

Pacific Northwest Indians, 21, 23, 37–48
pack baskets, *101*, 116
Paiute Indians, 55
palmetto strips, 194
Panamint Indians, 54, 55, *56*, 61
Papago Indians, 70–71
paper labels, 153
Passamaquoddy Indians, 89
patina, 153, 202
Penland, 175
Penn School, 192
Pennsylvania Dutch, 17, 155–62
Penobscot Indians, 89, 94, 116
Pequot Indians, 89
Pima Indians, 16, 70–71
plaited baskets, 20, 21, 71, 80
    Cherokee twill pattern, 84
plaques, Hopi, 71, 72, *75*
Pomo Indians, 17, 24, 50–53, *56*, 61, 62
porcupine work, 96
potlatch, 41, 45
pottery, 20, 69

Proper, Elizabeth, 141
Ptasvek, Nellie, *140*
pueblos, 68, 69, 71
Puritans, 102–3
purse basket, *143, 150*, 151

Qualla Arts and Crafts Mutual, Inc., 84
Quinault Indians, 45

raffia, 34–35
rattan baskets, 145, 150, 151
rattle-lid baskets, *15*,41
Ray, Charles B., 150
Ray, Clinton Mitchell ("Mitchy"), *143*,
    151, 153
Ray, Frederick, *146*
Reyes, José Formoso, *150*, 151
ribbed baskets, 77, 84, 170–71, *178*, 181
rice fanner, 188, 191
Rice Kingdom, 187–88, 191
Ritchie, Cordelia, *178, 179*, 185
river cane basketry, 79–80, 84, 85
rod basket, 171–72, *175*
Rosengarten, Dale, 195
Rossbach, Ed, 14–15
rush baskets, 188, 191
ryegrass, 32–33, 35
rye straw baskets, 158–160, 161

Sabbathday Lake, Maine, 120, 131
Saint Helena Island, S.C., 192
Salish culture, 38
Sam, Tootsie Dick, 62
Sandsbury, Andrew J., 150
Schagticoke Indians, 89, 94
Schaum, Joyce, *80, 125,* 193
Scots-Irish, 17, 164, 172
scrimshaw carvings, *150*, 151
seagrass baskets, *21, 187*, 188, 191, 192, 194, 197
Sea Islands, 188, 191–92
Sego, Nannie B., 185
Shakers, 17, 92, 119–34, 135, 199
    Taconic comparison, 136, 137, 140–41
skep basket, *155*, 159–60
Skokomish Indians, 45
Smithsonian Craft Show, 181
Smithsonian Institution, 61
Southeast Indians, 77–86
Southern Highland Handicraft Guild, 84–
    85, 185
South Union, Ky., 128
Southwest Indians, 15–16, 20, 21, 67–76
splint baskets
    Appalachia, 167
    New England settlers, 109
    Northeast Indians, 92–93, 96

Shaker, 124, 128, 135, 140–41
Southeast Indians, 80, 84
Taconic, 137, 140–41
split oak. *See* oak splint
Sprigg, June, 131
spruce root strips, 38, 39, 45
staves, *142*, 144–145, *150*
Stotler, Marie, *156*, 161
sumac baskets, 55, 75
swamp chestnut oak, 170
sweetgrass baskets, 192, 194
Sweetser, Gilman, 113, 116
swing-handled baskets, *136*, 137, 140, 145–
    46, *151*, 153
Sylvaro, Ferdinand, 153

Taconic area, 135–42
Taylor, Cynthia, 25, *170, 178*, 179, 181
Taylor, Nathan, 132
Tex, Julie, *64*
Thomas, Ada, 80
Tlingit Indians, 38, 39
totem poles, 38
Trail of Tears, 83
tray basket, *167*
twilled baskets, 84, 129
twined baskets, 20, 21
    Aleut, 33, *34, 35*
    Pomo, 51–52

Wallis, Birdie, 185
Walls, Jennifer Dawn, 178
Wampanoag Indians, 89, 142
Washburn, Newton, 113, 116
Washo Indians, 17, 50, 54, 55, 56
Watervliet, N.Y., 120
Western Apache, 70, 72, 75
West Taghkanic, N.Y., 137, 141
Wetherbee, Martha, 132, 141
whalers, 144, 145, 146
Whaley, Lydia, 185
white oak splint, 128, *167*, 170, 181
Whitney Museum of American Art, 131
willow baskets, 55, 70, 172, 178
winnowing basket, 103
Wood, David, 153
Wyer, Captain James, 150

Yakim, Aaron, *170, 178*, 179
Yokut Indians, 53, *56*
Youngblood, Mildred, 185
yucca, 71, 75
Yurok Indians, 61

Zeh, Stephen, 111, *113*, 116, 141, 193
Zuni Indians, 70

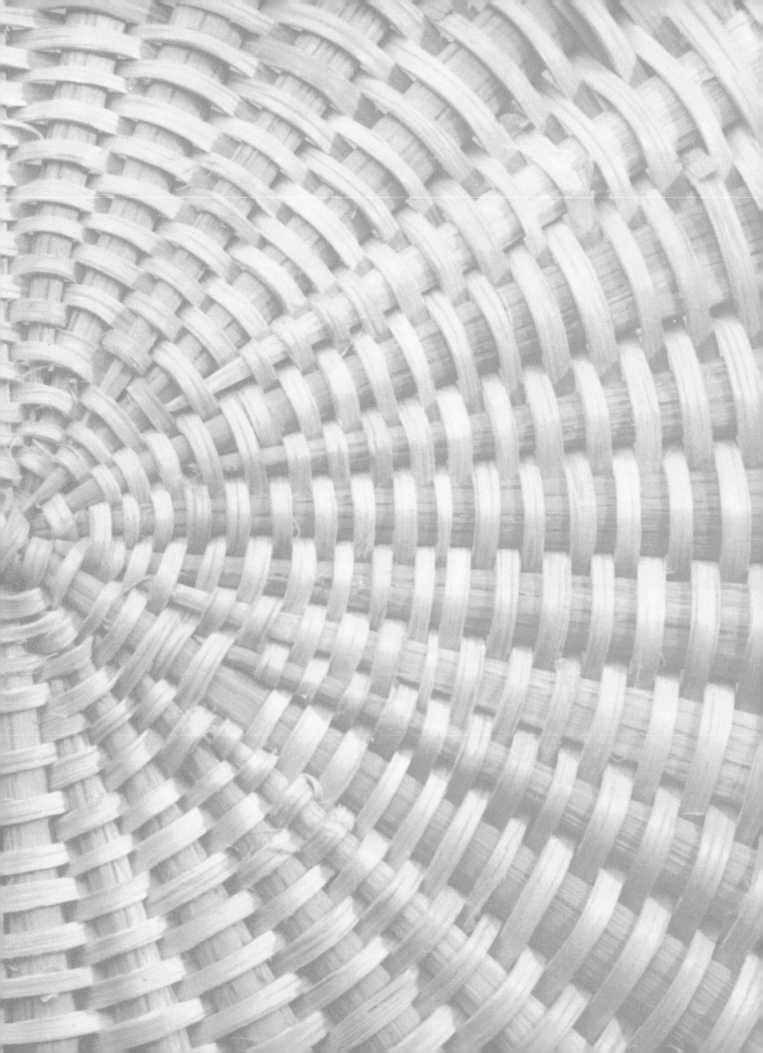

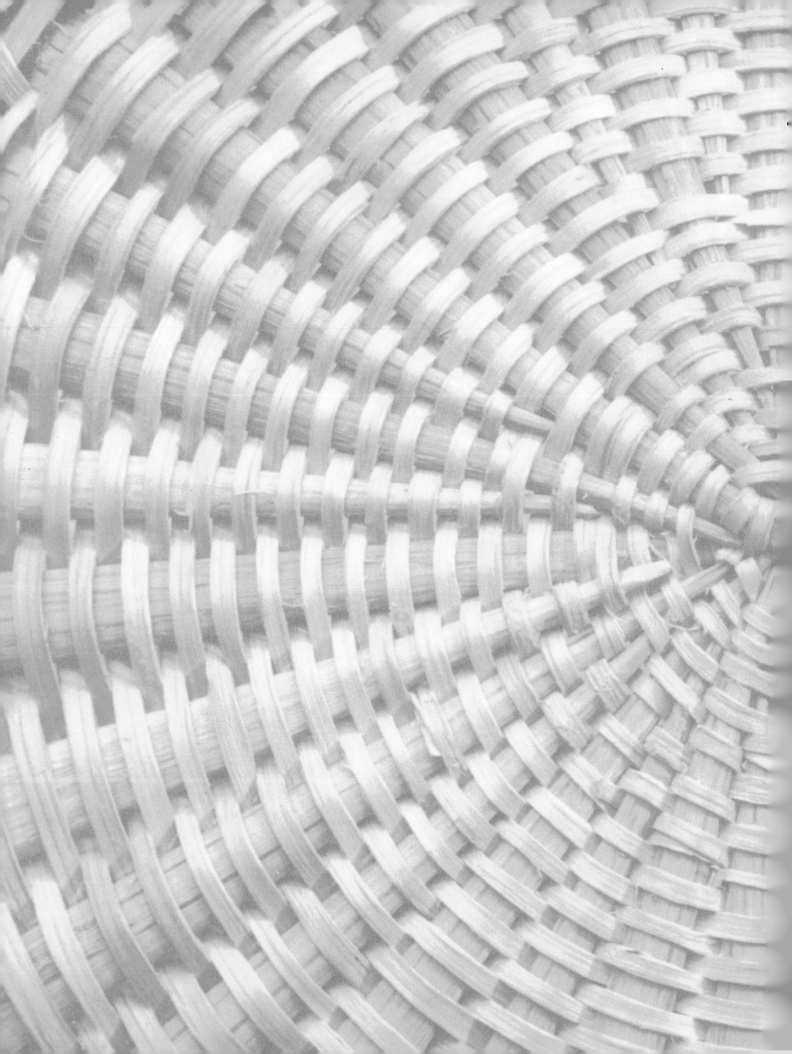